# GrandmotherTime

## JUDY GATTIS SMITH

Illustrations by Benjamin Vincent and Pam A. Allen

WORD PUBLISHING

Dallas·London·Vancouver·Melbourne

# Grandmother Time

Scripture quotations marked ICB are from the *International Children's Bible, New Century Version.* Copyright © 1983, 1986, 1988 by Word Publishing.

Scripture quotations marked NRSV are from the New Revised Standard Version Bible, copyright © 1989, by the Division of Christian Education of the National Council of the Churches of Christ in the United States of America.

**Library of Congress Cataloging-in-Publication Data**

Smith, Judy Gattis, 1933–
    Grandmother time / written by Judy Gattis Smith : illustrated
by Benjamin Vincent and Pam A. Allen.
       p.  cm.
    ISBN 0–8499–3249–1
    1. Christian education of children. 2. Grandparent and child.
I. Title.
    BV1475.2.S634   1991
    268'.085'3—dc 20            90–23794
                              CIP

Printed in the United States of America

1 2 3 4 9  LBM  9 8 7 6 5 4 3 2

For
Sarah Neel Smith
and
Laura Rush Scott

# CONTENTS

# Contents

## CHAPTER 7
**Grandmother Grace Notes** (with extra hints
especially for out-of-town grandmothers)

# INTRODUCTION

It is an awesome thing to be a grandmother. Seeing your child with a child calls you to consider the chain of life, the flow of God's creation. Memories mingle with anticipation of the future.

It is a celebrative thing to be a grandmother. Without the heavy responsibility of every moment with the child, a grandmother can sing and play and laugh and be silly. The grandmother, aware of the preciousness of fleeting childhood moments, can savor the time together.

For these moments this book was written. How short it all is, celebrating life together with those we love.

This book is a hodge-podge of many things that I, as a grandmother, wanted to share with you. There are stories, games, a letter, string tricks, Bible verses and "grandmother hints." It is not meant to be read straight through but picked up in a random fashion when you have "grandmother time" with your grandchildren.

It is my hope that these stories and activities will bring unique opportunities to impart our faith and Christian heritage to a most treasured generation.

*"Lord our Master, your name is the most wonderful name in all the earth! It brings you praise in heaven above. You have taught children and babies to sing praises to you" (Psalm 8:1–2, ICB\*).*

---

\* Two Bible translations are used throughout this book: International Children's Bible (ICB) and the New Revised Standard Version (NRSV).

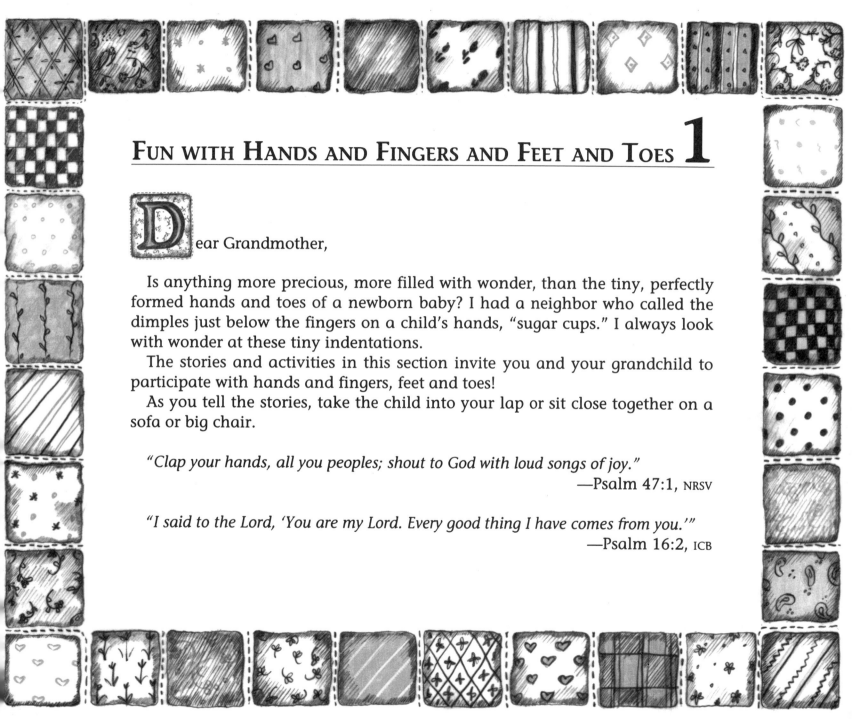

# Fun with Hands and Fingers and Feet and Toes 1

**D**ear Grandmother,

Is anything more precious, more filled with wonder, than the tiny, perfectly formed hands and toes of a newborn baby? I had a neighbor who called the dimples just below the fingers on a child's hands, "sugar cups." I always look with wonder at these tiny indentations.

The stories and activities in this section invite you and your grandchild to participate with hands and fingers, feet and toes!

As you tell the stories, take the child into your lap or sit close together on a sofa or big chair.

*"Clap your hands, all you peoples; shout to God with loud songs of joy."*
—Psalm 47:1, NRSV

*"I said to the Lord, 'You are my Lord. Every good thing I have comes from you.'"*
—Psalm 16:2, ICB

## THE SHEPHERD-KING

**This is a clapping story. As you read it aloud to your grandchildren, have them clap every time you say the words KING and SHEPHERD. If you say these words together, the children should clap twice. It can be challenging, especially for young children, not to clap at any other time. Read the story slowly at first. Then for fun you might like to read it faster and faster.**

Long ago there lived a man named Samuel. Samuel was a prophet who listened to God.

One day God said, "I am going to send you to Bethlehem to find a new KING (*clap*) for Israel. There is a man in Bethlehem named Jesse who has eight sons who are SHEPHERDS (*clap*). One of them will be the new KING (*clap*)—a SHEPHERD-KING (*clap-clap*)."

A great feast was prepared and the sons of Jesse came. First there was the oldest, Eliab, a SHEP-HERD (*clap*). He was tall and handsome. Samuel thought he would make a great KING (*clap*). But God said, "This is not the man. You want to choose him because of the way he looks. I care about the heart of my SHEPHERD-KING (*clap-clap*)."

Then Jesse brought his other sons to Samuel. They were all SHEPHERDS (*clap*). But Samuel shook his head. "God has chosen none of these to be KING (*clap*). Do you have another son? God is looking for a SHEPHERD-KING (*clap-clap*)."

Jesse said, "I have one more son, but I did not bring him to the feast. He is my youngest son and he is in the field, caring for my sheep."

Samuel told Jesse to send for the SHEPHERD-boy (*clap*) at once because God had chosen him to be KING (*clap*).

At last a rosy-cheeked, bright-eyed boy, dressed as a SHEPHERD (*clap*), arrived. The Lord said to Samuel, "This is the one I have chosen to be KING (*clap*)."

His name was David, the SHEPHERD-KING (*clap-clap*), and he became the leader of Israel.

## CLAPPING TO THE BOOKS OF THE BIBLE

**Young children have loved clapping to the "Pease Porridge Hot" rhyme for generations. Add some fun to learning the**

**books of the Bible by using the same type of clapping to accompany the book names:**

Grandmother and child face each other.
1. Touch lap with both hands flat, saying "Genesis" at the same time.
2. Clap hands together, saying "Exodus" at the same time.
3. Clap against outstretched hands of partner, saying "Leviticus" at the same time.
4. Clap hands together again, saying "Numbers" at the same time.
Keep repeating this pattern in rhythm.

**Eventually, add following books of the Bible in sets of four until all the books are memorized. A list of the books follows. Note that the Old and New Testaments each end in a three-book grouping. I suggest stretching the last books, Malachi and Revelation, to overlap Step 4 above (i.e., Mala-chi, Revela-tion). Now, as my grandchild always says, "Let's do it faster!"**

*Old Testament*

Genesis, Exodus, Leviticus, Numbers
Deuteronomy, Joshua, Judges, Ruth
1 Samuel, 2 Samuel, 1 Kings, 2 Kings
1 Chronicles, 2 Chronicles, Ezra, Nehemiah
Esther, Job, Psalms, Proverbs
Ecclesiastes, Song of Solomon, Isaiah, Jeremiah
Lamentations, Ezekiel, Daniel, Hosea
Joel, Amos, Obadiah, Jonah
Micah, Nahum, Habakkuk, Zephaniah
Haggai, Zechariah, Mala-chi

*New Testament*

Matthew, Mark, Luke, John
Acts, Romans, 1 Corinthians, 2 Corinthians
Galatians, Ephesians, Philippians, Colossians
1 Thessalonians, 2 Thessalonians, 1 Timothy, 2 Timothy
Titus, Philemon, Hebrews, James
1 Peter, 2 Peter, 1 John, 2 John
3 John, Jude, Revela-tion

## A PRAYERFUL HAND

**If you are with your grandchild at bedtime, gently massage the little hands. With very young children you can play a game to see what can wiggle—a thumb? a forefinger? Then use the hand as a five-finger reminder of prayer . . .**

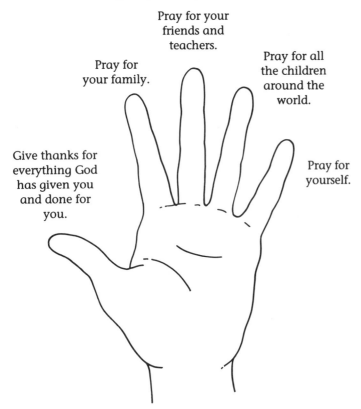

Pray for your friends and teachers.

Pray for your family.

Pray for all the children around the world.

Give thanks for everything God has given you and done for you.

Pray for yourself.

## THE STONE IN THE ROAD

**Here is something, just for fun, when your grandchild is learning "right" from "left." As this story is read, the child or children respond by raising the right hand every time the word THIS is said and by raising the left hand every time the word THAT is said. In addition, if the word KING is said, the child raises both hands and says, "Oh my!"**

THIS (*right hand*) is a story about a KING (*both hands, "Oh my!"*) who wanted his people to learn to do things for themselves. When a problem came up they always said, "Should we do THIS (*right*) or THAT (*left*)?" or, "Let's ask the KING (*both, 'Oh my!'*)."

THAT (*left*) would cause a problem. "Why can't they do either THIS (*right*) or THAT (*left*) and not always ask me?" the KING (*both, "Oh my!"*) said. "I think it is time to teach them a lesson."

So the KING (*both, "Oh my!"*) called his trusted servant. "Take THIS (*right*) shovel and THAT (*left*) pick and dig a hole in the middle of the road. Take THAT (*left*) gold. Put it in THIS (*right*) bag and hide it in THAT (*left*) hole and cover it with THAT (*left*) dirt," said the King (*both, "Oh my!"*).

"Then push THIS (*right*) rock over THAT (*left*) hole so it cannot be seen." The servant did as he was told.

"Now," the KING (*both, "Oh my!"*) said, "whoever moves THAT (*left*) rock out of the middle of THIS (*right*) road may keep the gold."

After a while a man came along. "What's THIS (*right*)?" he asked. "What is a rock like THIS (*right*) doing in a place like THAT (*left*)? THIS (*right*) will never do. THIS (*right*) rock will block my cart when I take my vegetables to the market. I must go and tell the KING (*both, 'Oh my!'*)."

"THIS (*right*) is just what I expected," said the King (*both, "Oh my!"*). "THAT (*left*) man will not get the gold."

It went on like THIS (*right*) for days. Everyone commented on the rock but no one moved it.

One day a young boy came down the road. "What's THIS (*right*)? A big rock in the middle of the road? THAT (*left*) is dangerous. Someone might get hurt. I'll see if I can move it! THAT's (*left*) it. I did it. Now no one will get hurt. But, what's THIS (*right*)? A bag of gold? I must return THAT (*left*) to the KING (*both, 'Oh my!'*)."

But the KING (*both, "Oh my!"*) had been watching all of THIS (*right*). "At last I've found someone who can do THIS (*right*) or THAT (*left*) for himself!" he said.

The boy said, "Sir, anyone could do THIS (*right*) or THAT (*left*)."

The KING (*both, "Oh my!"*) replied, "Anyone could do THIS (*right*) or THAT (*left*), but only you did it. Only you moved the stone. THIS (*right*) gold is yours."

And THAT's (*left*) the end of THIS (*right*) story about THAT (*left*) boy and THAT (*left*) gold and the KING (*both, "Oh my!"*).

# Listen

Words and music by Mary Lu Walker

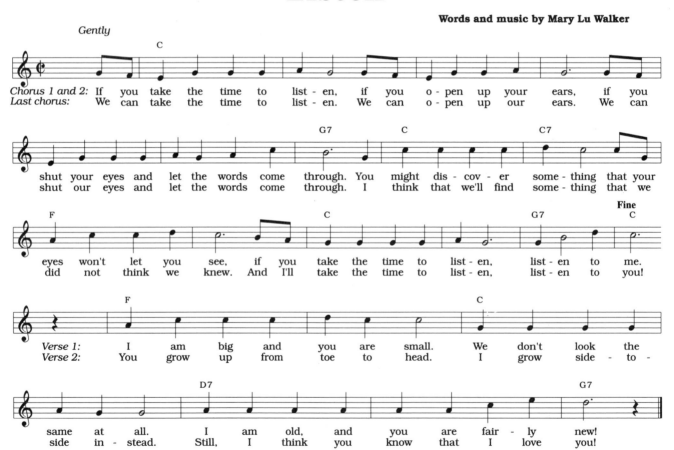

*Gently*

**Chorus 1 and 2:** If you take the time to list-en, if you o-pen up your ears, if you

**Last chorus:** We can take the time to list-en. We can o-pen up our ears. We can

shut your eyes and let the words come through. You might dis-cov-er some-thing that your

shut our eyes and let the words come through. I think that we'll find some-thing that we

eyes won't let you see, if you take the time to list-en, list-en to me.

did not think we knew. And I'll take the time to list-en, list-en to you!

**Verse 1:** I am big and you are small. We don't look the

**Verse 2:** You grow up from toe to head. I grow side - to -

same at all. I am old, and you are fair - ly new!

side in - stead. Still, I think you know that I love you!

## GRANDMOTHER JUDY'S TOE STORIES

**When my granddaughter Sarah Neel was a baby, like most children, she loved the rhyme, "This Little Pig Went to Market." She would chortle and giggle as her toes were wiggled. At a very early age she would say "wee, wee, wee" with the littlest pig.**

**As she grew older, the "Little Pigs" rhyme was too babyish. Quite accidentally one day I discovered that there are a number of Bible stories that use ten people. These became "Grandmother Judy's Toe Stories."**

**There is something very intimate and relaxing about massaging feet and toes. By cultivating an atmosphere that is serene and caring, we can teach a Bible story in a very special way.**

*Toe Story #1: Ten Men Spoiled God's Plan*

**Get in a comfortable position with the child's bare feet in your lap. Begin by kneading the feet. Work with your thumbs and fingertips between the small bones of the child's foot. Also use long, firm strokes down the length of the child's foot.**

You remember how Moses led the people from Israel out of Egypt. As our story begins, they were leaving the dreary desert behind and were very near Canaan, a land which God had promised to give them for their own country.

Their feet were probably very tired and burning after all that walking across hot, desert sands.

Only one more march forward would take them across the border and into the beautiful country. They took down their tents, and the cloud they had been following began to move forward. But then the people became afraid.

"We don't know what lies ahead of us."

"Our feet hurt."

"We don't want to go."

"Let's send some men ahead to spy on the land. When they come back they can tell us what they have seen and which is the best way for us to go."

(*Now, give a special push with your thumb every time you say the word FORGOT.*) They FORGOT how God had always led them in the past. They FORGOT the miracles God had done before Pharaoh, the King. They FORGOT how the Red Sea had parted. They FORGOT how God had saved their lives by giving them water out of a rock. They FORGOT about the manna, their food from heaven.

Now the people from Israel wanted to depend on themselves. And God let them. God told Moses to choose twelve men, and send them to search the land carefully. They were to spy on the land of Canaan.

For forty days the spies went throughout the promised land. They saw the land was beautiful and had lots of good food.

At the end of forty days, they returned to Israel's camp. They brought samples of huge fruit. The Israelites had never seen such wonderful fruit.

Then ten of the spies began to tell about the land.

(*Now, simply wiggle each toe. Begin with the big toe, right foot.*) The first spy said, "It is a good country, but the people are stronger than we are."

(*Go to the second toe.*) The second spy said. "They live in cities with great walls that reach the sky."

(*Third toe.*) The third spy said, "They are like giants—so powerful and tall that to them we look like grasshoppers."

(*Fourth toe.*) The fourth spy said, "They have strange, powerful weapons."

(*Little toe.*) The fifth spy said, "God can't help us against them."

(*Switch to the left foot.*) And the next five spies repeated just what the others had said:

(*Big toe, left foot.*) "Too strong."

(*Second toe.*) "Great walls."

(*Third toe.*) "Too big."

(*Fourth toe.*) "Great weapons."

(*Little toe.*) "God won't help us."

(*Now wiggle all the toes vigorously.*) "No! No! No! We can't go! We will all be killed!"

Two of the spies, Caleb and Joshua, said, "Don't be afraid. We can do it. Come on! Let's go now!"

But the people listened to the ten other spies and believed them. "We'd rather die in the desert than be killed by giants."

And because the people did not obey and go to Canaan, God would not allow them to go to the good land God had promised them. No one who was twenty years old and older, except Joshua and Caleb, would ever get to live in Canaan. The people from Israel had to go back into the dreary desert and camp there until every man who had not trusted God had died.

Then their children could go to Canaan, God's promised land.

(*Wiggle each toe one last time.*) And that is how ten little spies spoiled God's plan for Israel.

*Toe Story #2: The Ten Lepers*

**As during the first toe story, get in a comfortable position with the child's bare feet in your lap.**

Jesus and His disciples were walking, walking, walking one day from Capernaum to Jerusalem. (*Grasp the toes with one hand and the ankle with your other. Gently rotate the whole foot back and forth.*) Walking, walking, walking from Capernaum to Jerusalem. (*Do the same with the other foot.*)

Ten men who had a bad skin disease called leprosy saw Jesus and his disciples passing by. They had heard about how Jesus had healed other people with their disease so they cried out loudly to Him. (*Wiggle big toe, right foot.*) "Help us!"

(*Second toe.*) "Heal us!"

(*Third toe.*) "Cure us!"

(*Fourth toe.*) "Save us!"

(*Little toe.*) "Please, please, please!"

(*Switch to the left foot. Wiggle big toe, left foot.*) "Help us!"

(*Second toe.*) "Heal us!"

(*Third toe.*) "Cure us!"

(*Fourth toe.*) "Save us!"

(*Little toe.*) "Please, please, please!"

Jesus never refused to help anyone who asked Him with a sincere heart. So, He stopped and went to the ten lepers and told them to go and show themselves to the priest.

(*Grasp the top part of all the toes of one foot using your thumb and fingers. Rotate clockwise and counterclockwise.*)

They all left at once to go see the priests. And as they went, the bad skin disease left their bodies and they were made completely well.

(*Do the same as above with the other foot.*)

The lepers continued on their way. The one who had called, "Help us!" did not come back and thank Jesus. (*Wiggle big toe, right foot.*)

The one who had cried, "Heal us!" did not come back and thank Jesus. (*Wiggle second toe.*)

The one who had said, "Cure us!" did not come back and thank Jesus. (*Wiggle third toe.*)

The one who had said, "Save us!" did not come back and thank Jesus. (*Wiggle fourth toe.*)

But the one who had said, "Please, please, please!" stopped and turned around. He ran back to Jesus and fell down and thanked Him. (*Wiggle little toe.*)

Jesus asked, "Where are the others? (*Switch to the left foot.*)

"The one who had called, 'Help us!' did not come back and thank me. (*Wiggle big toe, left foot.*)

"The one who had cried, 'Heal us!' did not come back and thank me. (*Wiggle second toe.*)

"The one who had cried, 'Cure us!' did not come back and thank me. (*Wiggle third toe.*)

"The one who had said, 'Save us!' did not come back and thank me. (*Wiggle fourth toe.*)

"Only the one who had said, 'Please, please, please!' came back and thanked me." (*Wiggle little toe.*)

Then Jesus said to the man kneeling at His feet,

# The Toes of Mary Rose

**Words and music by Mary Lu Walker**

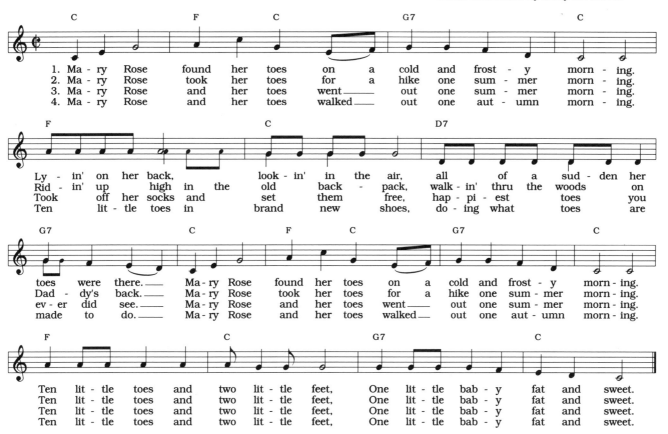

1. Ma-ry Rose found her toes on a cold and frost-y morn-ing.
2. Ma-ry Rose took her toes for a hike one sum-mer morn-ing.
3. Ma-ry Rose and her toes went out one sum-mer morn-ing.
4. Ma-ry Rose and her toes walked out one au-tumn morn-ing.

Ly-in' on her back, look-in' in the air, all of a sud-den her
Rid-in' up high in the old back-pack, walk-in' thru the woods on
Took off her socks and set them free, hap-pi-est toes you
Ten lit-tle toes in brand new shoes, do-ing what toes are

toes were there. Ma-ry Rose found her toes on a cold and frost-y morn-ing.
Dad-dy's back. Ma-ry Rose took her toes for a hike one sum-mer morn-ing.
ev-er did see. Ma-ry Rose and her toes went out one sum-mer morn-ing.
made to do. Ma-ry Rose and her toes walked out one au-tumn morn-ing.

Ten lit-tle toes and two lit-tle feet, One lit-tle bab-y fat and sweet.
Ten lit-tle toes and two lit-tle feet, One lit-tle bab-y fat and sweet.
Ten lit-tle toes and two lit-tle feet, One lit-tle bab-y fat and sweet.
Ten lit-tle toes and two lit-tle feet, One lit-tle bab-y fat and sweet.

## Nurturing by Nature

**D**ear Grandmother,

Outdoors with our grandchildren is such a special place to be. As we walk together in parks, examine rocks and pause in awe of butterflies, we are constantly more aware of the beauties of God's world and of the many ways God has gifted us.

The child is often the teacher here—marveling over buds on trees, slants of light, the intricate beauty of a sea shell. We become aware of a God who cares and loves us deeply.

Through the eyes of a child, the edge has not been taken off the glory of God's creation. Everything is new and delightful.

*"The earth is the Lord's and all that is in it, the world, and those who live in it; for he has founded it on the seas, and established it on the rivers."*

—Psalm 24:1–2, NRSV

## MORNING GLORIES AND EVENING STORIES

**Take advantage of special times outdoors to tell Bible stories. Early in the morning before anyone else gets up, a child may awake and come looking for Grandmother. This is a delightful time to go outdoors. While the rosy glow of sunrise has in it the flaming glory of creation, tell your grandchild the wonderful story of how the world began . . .**

Long, long ago there was no world at all. But even then there was God. Think back, back to the beginning of time. This was when God made the world. At first, darkness was everywhere—like the sky looked today before the sun started coming up. God planned the world to be beautiful so God separated light and darkness and called them "day" and "night." Wasn't that a wonderful idea—to create two beautiful times—day and night?

And then God made the beautiful blue sky. Look as high and as far as you can into the sky above you. God called the sky "heaven." Then God thought we needed earth and seas and mountains, and just like that, God created them!

But there was nothing on the earth—just plain earth—so God dressed it with a carpet of green grass and beautiful flowers and trees and bushes. God thought this was very good, and it was.

But our God who creates and creates wasn't through yet. God made stars to twinkle and moonbeams to glimmer and a powerful sun to rise just as we see it rising now with bands of beautiful color. How many colors can you see?

Next God began to make living creatures. God made every kind of fish—gigantic whales and fish so tiny your eyes cannot even see them without a microscope. And God made colorful birds to fly and sing. Listen now. Hear the birds singing "Good Morning" to God? God was pleased with them all. The earth was becoming more and more beautiful just as God had planned.

Then God had the great idea of making animals—all the animals, big and little, creeping and running. There was suddenly life everywhere, in the woods and on the plains, on the tops of mountains and in the bottoms of caves—LIFE! And the animals ran free and praised God.

Then God wished to have people live in the wonderful world that was created. God made a man and a woman who could enjoy this beautiful world and understand who had made all these great things. And the man and woman could love and worship God.

Now everything was in place just like God wanted.

Every day the sun rises just like this, and we can look at it and remember this story of how the world began and think about our wonderful God who made it all.

**We are storytelling people. Some of our earliest Bible stories were told in the evening around campfires, even before people could write.**

**Nighttime when the stars are out is still a great time to tell Bible stories. Try to slip away into the outdoors in the early evening with your grandchild.**

**As you look up in the dark night sky, you might want to tell the story of the three wise men who studied the stars . . .**

The wise men knew all the stars. But one night they discovered a new star in the sky, one they had never seen before. God caused them to know by this star that Jesus, the long-awaited Savior, had been born.

The wise men wanted to see this baby, and they set out to follow the star. For many, many nights they traveled, setting their course by that star which moved slowly before them as if leading them to the right place.

When they reached Bethlehem, the star stood still over the place where Mary and Joseph were staying. There they found the wonderful child they had read about. The child was baby Jesus.

## A ROCK PARADE

*"The Lord says, 'Listen to me, those of you who try to live right and follow the Lord. Look at the rock from which you were cut'"* (Isaiah 51:1, ICB).

**What fun it is to have a rock parade with your grandchild! Just go with your grand-children to a rocky area and send them off to find favorite stones or pebbles. Perhaps you have pebbles in your own yard.**

**When a small pile has been assembled, look the rocks over. Have the children point out features and shapes and then draw faces on the stones with tempera paint and brushes or felt-tipped markers.**

**You can even help your grandchildren trace their family tree by letting them**

create their own family of rock people. Then line up your rock family in a parade. The children of course lead the parade, followed by parents and grandparents. You, as a grandmother, can tell your grandchildren about your parents and grandparents and help the children represent them as rock people and add them to the parade.

You might try making a rock parade of our biblical ancestors. How many can you name? There were Abraham and Sarah, then Isaac and Rebekah—you may want to consult your Bible or Bible storybook.

Another idea is to just let the children create rock people from as many Bible characters as they know (for example, Noah, David, Moses, Ruth, Daniel) and then see if they can line them up in chronological order. This is especially fun with older grandchildren.

## SIMPLE PLEASURES

There are many simple pleasures in nature that are quick and fun to enjoy without special tools or equipment. Every part of the country has its own unique natural characteristics. Point out these local plants, animals, sounds and objects to your grandchild.

Long, pleasant moments can be spent with your grandchild blowing the furry seed-heads off mature dandelions. Tell the child that a blessing is a special wish. Encourage the child to send a blessing to someone special and then blow the blessing to them on the wings of the dandelion seed-heads.

There are many funny and intriguing things in nature for those who have eyes to see. Go with your grandchild to look for faces in flowers. Pansies and Johnny-jump-ups offer endless possibilities. What a funny thing—to look at a flower and see it looking back at you.

Pussy willows are a special plant for feeling—very softly and gently. Did you know there is a tiny early spring wildflower called pussytoes? By looking close to the ground in wooded areas you might discover this plant which is equally delightful to stroke gently.

Most children love to go on hunts. Go on a treasure hunt in the woods to find a sassafras tree. It has three different kinds of leaves and some are shaped like mittens.

You don't have to do anything special with nature objects. Looking is the most interesting of all. There are intriguing field flowers almost everywhere in nature. Get a book of wildflowers in your area and set off with your grandchild for a great adventure. It is pleasant to be reminded that we are looking at the same flowers and calling them by the same vivid names as early Americans did. These same flowers grow plentifully along the sides of our roads today—in my area of the country, we have snake plant, crowfoot, cowbane and butterfly weed. You may have bluebonnets, Indian paintbrush, morning glory or a variety of other wildflowers.

Pick an object in nature and you and your grandchild try to imitate it. Perhaps it is a large rock. Sit very still. Let your body be quiet and solid like the rock. Perhaps it is a tree. Stand as the tree is standing. Let your arms be branches. Be still or move very slowly as the tree does, swaying as if caught in gentle breezes or strong winds. Pick a flower and just stare at it with your mind blank, relaxed and deeply

satisfied, treasuring the moment with this special person—your grandchild.

Sit quietly and listen to nature's sounds which are often soft and subtle. Can the children identify the sounds? A bird? An insect? A rustling of leaves? Each of you hold up a finger when you hear a new sound.

Find a tree to lie under. In the spring watch the buds come out. In the autumn watch the leaves fall. In the summer see how many shades of green you can identify. Make this just a quiet time that the two of you can share. Look at the tree through unhurried, careful eyes. Absorb all that is going on around you: wonder and dream.

Sometimes we can pick an object from nature and make something. To pick a leaf or a flower should not hurt most plants. You will not destroy it if you are careful. How many of you remember these simple nature activities from your childhood? It's fun to share them with your grandchildren:

Make a crown of daisies.
Make a clover-chain necklace.

Play "He loves me/He loves me not" with the petals of a daisy.

Powder your nose with a buttercup. Does it leave your nose yellow?

Put acorn tops on your fingers as hats for finger people.

Put geranium petals on your fingernails. Lick the underside and stick them on.

Suck the nectar from a honeysuckle blossom.

Make a blade of grass whistle.

Make milkweed-pod boats. Twirl and dance through the flying milkweed seeds.

Cut an apple horizontally and discover the star inside.

## TRAIL TALES

**Make a "story-map" for wherever you live or travel. Draw a map including interesting things you saw on a recent vacation, business trip, or even a visit downtown. Then explain to your grandchild the different points of interest. This is yet another way to share with your grandchildren the wonders of our world. Here's an example (the map is to the right):**

My Dear Grandchild,

I wish you could have been with me today. Come along in your imagination, and we'll take an autumn walk along the Appalachian Trail.

Clue box:

1. I started here on the edge of the woods. The wildflowers were all purple and yellow. There were tall weeds and lacy goldenrods. The blossoms of one plant looked like little purple bells.

2. It was rocky here and a little slippery. Oops! Glad I had my hiking stick.

3. A chipmunk ran right across the path here.

4. The first leaves were just beginning to change colors. There were a few deep red leaves on this oak tree.

5. Something red caught my eye here. Almost hidden were bright-red fall berries.

6. I was high enough here to look around. There were mountain ranges in layers of blue like lumpy blankets piled on top of each other.

7. I had to cross a stream here by stepping carefully on river rocks.

8. Time for lunch on a sun-warmed rock with a long-distance view. I looked as far as I could see in the direction where you live.

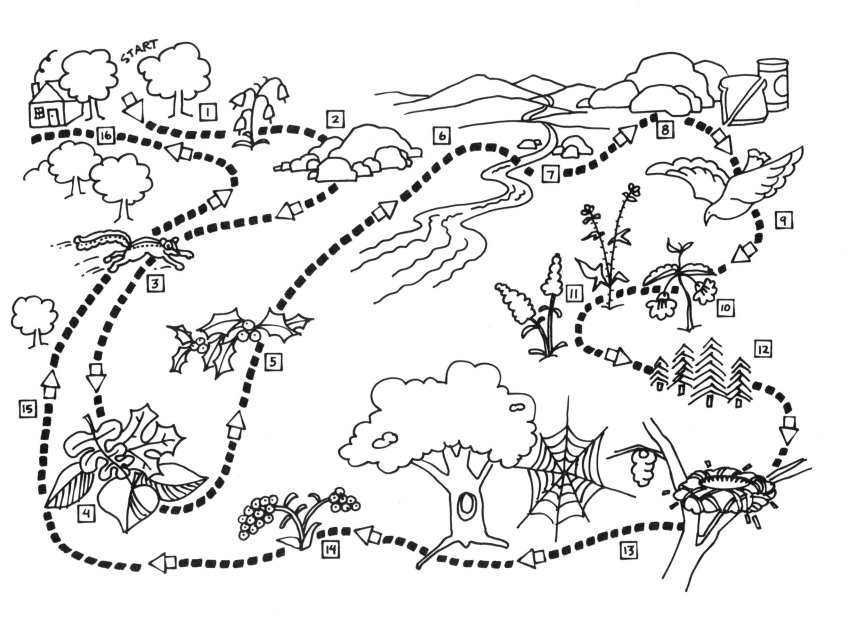

START

9. I saw a falcon swooping and dancing in the sky here. They are coming back to this area.

10. A hillside of jewelweed! These yellow flowers pop when you touch them. Another name is touch-me-not.

11. I stopped here and looked at some plants with funny names. "Tear-thumb" has a stem as sharp as a razor blade. No wonder it is called "tear-thumb." And I saw some "heal-all"—I wonder what this small purple flower heals!

12. I went through a hemlock forest here. It was cool and dark. The ground was covered with good-smelling pine needles.

13. I found some animal homes here—a nest, a cocoon, a web, a hole in a tree. Can you tell me who lives in each of these?

14. What a surprise! A beautiful "doll's eye" plant. There are lots of white berries on a stem with a block dot on each berry—just like the glass eyes of dolls!

15. Back to the red-leaf oak tree, back past the chipmunk path, back down the rocky climb, back to the purple and gold roadside flowers.

16. Time to go home, refreshed and renewed by some special hours in God's beautiful world.

## A LITTLE IMAGINATION

**We as grandmothers often have the time that busy parents do not have to cultivate the imagination of a child. The following verses are imagination-stretchers that attempt to create word pictures thought-provoking to a child. Share them outdoors and let the child run and find each nature object suggested. Allow time for daydreaming after each verse.**

*Every child needs a pebble—a bit of nature's mountains.*
*Go right now and find one. Hold it in your hand.*
*Smooth and black or grey and rough with sparkles and cracks.*
*Let it speak to you of high snowy mountains,*
*ocean shores, rocky beaches far away,*
*Indian arrowheads, ancient forts.*
*Look at your pebble.*
*What do you see?*

(Allow time for daydreaming.)

*Every child needs a blade of grass—a bit of nature's prairies.*
*Go right now and find one. Hold it in your hand.*
*Let it speak to you of haystacks and harvest, of fields of grass*
*hiding millions of moving things—fantastic webs and tangles,*
*marching armies of ants, spiders,*
*tiny things with tiny homes.*
*Feel the sharp edges. Run your fingers around them.*
*What do you see?*

(Allow time for daydreaming.)

*Every child needs a new green leaf—a bit of nature's jungles.*
*Go right now and find one. Hold it in your hand.*
*Let it speak to you of steaming jungles,*
*chattering monkeys and brilliant parrots,*
*of vines fighting for the sunlight, curling, twisting,*
*of high things, green things, twenty-six shades of green.*
*Smell it. Touch it.*
*What do you see?*

(Allow time for daydreaming.)

*Every child needs a twig of wood—a bit of nature's forests.*
*Go right now and find one. Hold it in your hand.*
*Let it speak to you of giant redwoods stretching to the sky,*
*of log bridges over roaring waters,*
*crackling campfires, ancient warships.*
*Rub it. Stroke it.*
*Look and listen.*
*What do you see?*

(Allow time for daydreaming.)

*By holding in our hands*
*the tiniest pieces of nature,*
*God shows us a glimpse of fantastic worlds,*
*fantastic times gone by.*
*There is so much to see.*
*Stretch your minds. Think big thoughts.*
*Open the eyes of your heart.*
*Look, listen and dream.*

## STRINGS AND THINGS

Dear Grandmother,

As I was growing up, my grandmother taught me to do string tricks, and my grandfather made wonderful shadow-pictures on the wall. In these days of TV and videos, those simple pleasures seem lost. Why not revive them for that special time with your grandchild?

*"I will speak using stories. I will tell things that have been secret since long ago."*
—Psalm 78:2, ICB

## STRING TRICK STORIES

**All over the world string figures have been used to pass on traditions and stories.**

**This is a fun experience to have with your grandchildren as they reach elementary age. They may have already picked up some of the traditional patterns at school. Now you can use these patterns to tell and reinforce familiar Bible stories. For example, "cat's cradle" can become Moses' cradle in the bulrushes and "fishnet," also called "Jacob's ladder," can be used to tell the story of Jacob's dream.**

**First you will need string. Plain kitchen string, butcher's string, or macramé or nylon cord can be used. Tie about six feet of string into a loop.**

**Practice the Basic Position, Position 1 and Opening A as follows:**

### The Basic Position

Your hands begin in the basic position for most string figures and usually return to the basic position after each move.

1. In the Basic Position, your hands are parallel, palms facing each other, fingers pointing up.

You will notice the hands in some of the pictures are not in the basic position. These hands are shown with the palms facing out so that you can see each step more clearly.

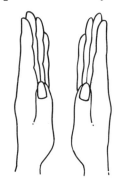

*Position 1*

1. With your hands in the basic position, hang the loop of string on your thumbs. Stretch your hands as far apart as you can to make the string loop taut.
2. Pick up the far thumb string with your little fingers. The string that goes across the palm of your hand is called the palmar string.

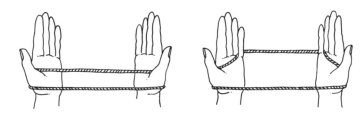

*Opening A*

Many string figures begin with Opening A.

1. Put the string loop on your fingers as in Position 1.
2. With your right index finger, pick up from below the palmar string on your left hand, and return to the basic position, pulling this string on the back of your index finger as far as it will go.

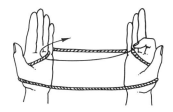

3. With your left index finger, pick up the right palmar string, from below, in between the strings of the loop that goes around your right index finger. Return to the basic position, again pulling out the palmar string as far as it will go.

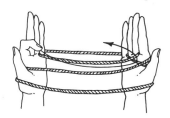 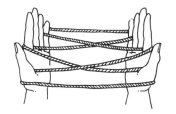

**Now we are ready to combine stories and figures . . .**

## BABY MOSES

The people from Israel were living as slaves in Egypt. A wicked King ruled the land, and he became afraid that the Israelites would become powerful and take over his land.

This King wished to have new cities built where he could store his rich treasures, so he commanded the Israelites to build those cities. He made them carry heavy stones and backbreaking loads of bricks. He placed slave masters over the workers to make them work very hard and very fast. But the harder they worked the stronger they grew and Pharaoh saw that his plan was not working.

"I'll make life even more miserable for them," he said. "Every baby boy that is born to an Israelite must be thrown into the Nile River.

After this horrible command had been put into practice, baby Moses was born.

For three months his mother was able to hide him. But every day soldiers rode by her house looking for baby boys. It became harder and harder to hide baby Moses. Then she thought of a very wise plan.

First she gathered bulrushes (plants which grew along the side of the river). Then she wove a little basket like this:

(*Here do the "Baby Moses' Cradle" string trick with your grandchild.*)

When it was finished, she made a soft bed in the basket and placed the baby in it. Carefully she placed the basket near the edge of the river among the tall reeds. Moses' sister Miriam watched Moses in his basket.

(*Rock the cradle on your fingers as if waves were lapping around it.*)

This story has a happy ending. A princess found the baby Moses and took him home to the King's palace to raise him. And Moses' very own mother became his nurse. Moses was right where God wanted him to be.

(*Repeat the story, letting the child tell it to you.*)

### Baby Moses' Cradle

1. Put the string loop around the backs of the fingers (but not the thumb) of each hand.

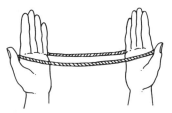

2. Your right index finger and thumb pick up the near string of the loop around your left hand and wrap it once around your left hand. The string comes out between your left index finger and thumb. Then your left index finger and thumb pick up the near string of the loop around your right hand and wrap it once around your right hand. Make sure you always pick up the near string.

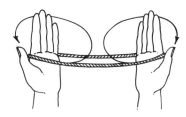

3. Now complete as in Opening A using your *middle* fingers.

4. This is Baby Moses' Cradle.

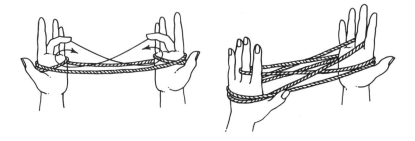

## DANIEL IN THE LION'S DEN

**This story uses the string trick, "Lion's Whiskers." Practice it until you feel comfortable doing it. Then tell the story, inserting the string trick.**

Daniel was a young man who lived long ago. Daniel always tried to be honest and truthful and obey God. He lived in the land of Babylon because the people where he had lived had been taken as captives from their own land. The Bible says Daniel had "an excellent Spirit in him," so the King of the land, King Darius, liked him very much. Soon Daniel was more highly honored than any other governor or president in the land.

A bitter feeling of jealousy began to grow in the hearts of the other governors and presidents. Because these men knew that Daniel prayed three times a day to God and praised God, they came up with a wicked plan. They tricked the King into signing a law that said that for thirty days, no one could pray to anyone except the King or they would be thrown into a den of lions. The King was flattered by this idea. He thought the people just wanted to honor him. So he signed the law.

But Daniel loved God and continued to pray to God. So the wicked men happily reported it to the King.

The King was very upset. He did not want to hurt Daniel. He tried all day to find ways to change the law he had made, but he could not. The King understood after it was too late, that he had been tricked into making the law.

That evening, the governors and presidents came to the King demanding that the law be obeyed. King Darius sadly realized he had no other choice.

Daniel was put in a large, dark pit, and a stone was rolled across the entrance. As his eyes became accustomed to the darkness, something began to take shape. (*Follow "Lion's Whiskers" steps 1–9.*) He saw the whiskers on the face of a large lion. (*Drop the string. Resume Opening A again.*) Then he saw, in another corner, another lion. (*Do the string trick again. Create as many lions as you like.*) But the lions were quiet and seemed almost gentle.

Inside the palace the King stayed awake all night, refusing to eat and praying for his friend Daniel.

Early the next morning, King Darius ran to the lion's den. There was Daniel, safe and unharmed. King Darius was so happy. Quickly, he took Daniel out of the pit.

Then King Darius believed in God. He wrote letters to the people of every nation telling them about the wonderful way in which God had delivered Daniel from the lions.

*(Teach your grandchild the string trick, and then let him or her tell the story back to you.)*

### Lion's Whiskers

1. Do Opening A.
2. Your thumbs drop their loops.

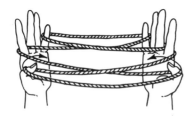

3. Turn your hands away from you with the palms facing out and the thumbs facing down.
4. Your thumbs pick up from below the far little finger string (the bottom string), and return under the strings of the index loops.

5. Your thumbs go over the near index string to get the far index strings and return.

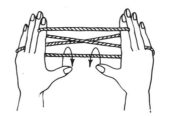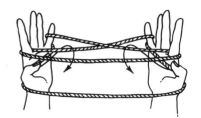

6. You little fingers drop their loops.
7. Your little fingers go over the near index strings to get the near thumb strings and return.

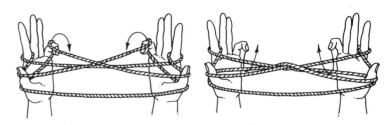

8. Your thumbs drop their loops.
9. This is Lion's Whiskers.

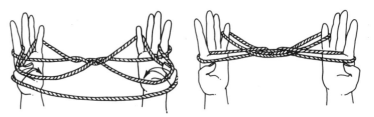

## JACOB'S DREAM

**This story uses the string trick known as "fishnet" or "Jacob's Ladder." To do this trick follow the directions for "Lion's Whiskers" in the previous story, "Daniel in the Lion's Den," and then add steps 10-17 as follows. When you have mastered the trick, tell this story:**

Jacob had done a terrible thing. He had cheated his own twin brother out of his family inheritance. Jacob had disguised himself and pretended to be his brother, Esau. Their father was very old and blind, and he gave the family inheritance to Jacob instead of Esau.

When Esau found out about it, he was very mad! In fact he was so mad, Jacob was afraid Esau would kill him.

And so Jacob ran away from home. He felt guilty and frightened and lonely.

One evening after a long, tiring day of walking and running, Jacob lay down on the ground to go to sleep. For a pillow he used a large stone.

While Jacob slept he had a wonderful dream. He saw a ladder set on the earth which reached all the way to heaven.

*(Create the string trick, "Jacob's Ladder.")*

In Jacob's dream angels were going up and down the ladder, and at the top of the ladder stood God! Wouldn't that be a wonderful dream?

In Jacob's dream, God spoke. God told Jacob, "I am with you and will protect you everywhere you go. And I will give you and your family this land."

Jacob woke up. What a comfort it was to him to know that God was with him, even though he believed he didn't deserve God's love. And God promises the same thing to us. God will always be with us and love us.

### Jacob's Ladder

10. Your thumbs go over both strings of the index loops to get the near little finger strings and return.

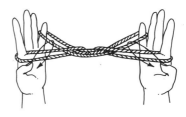

11. Use your right thumb and index finger to pull out the left index loop and share it with your left thumb. Do this again to share the right index loop with your right thumb.

12. Tip your thumbs under the near string and return.

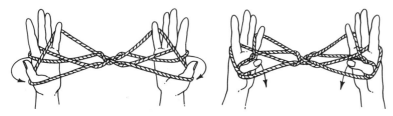

13. Near each thumb there is a string triangle. Your index fingers go down into these triangles.

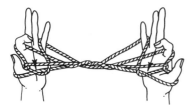

14. Gently take your little fingers out of their loops.

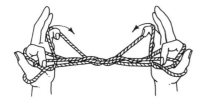

15. Turn your hands so that the palms face away from you. Don't worry about the index loops. They will just slip off your index fingers.

16. Your index fingers straighten up and extend the "fishnet."

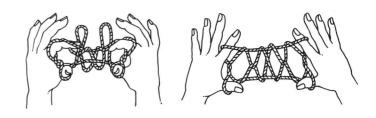

17. Tilt your hands vertically to make "Jacob's Ladder."

## SHADOW PLAY

**From "hand-made" shadows on the wall, you can create a variety of animal shapes. Use these creatures to add life to favorite Bible stories and Bible verses. Some of the ones included, such as the camel and sheep, are challenging to form. Others even a youngster will have fun shadowing—like the dog, rabbit, duck and crocodile. You will need a light behind you, a wall on which to reflect the shadows and nimble fingers.**

## CAMELS CHOOSE A WIFE

**Study the following illustration and experiment until you can create a camel. Then tell this story using the camel character.**

When Isaac lived long, long ago, it was the custom for parents to choose wives for their sons. Though Isaac had a great faith in God, he lived in a land where most people did not worship God. So his father, Abraham, was very worried about how he would find a good wife for his son. Abraham knew that far away in Haran there were people who worshiped God. So he had an idea. He would send his trusted servant Eliezer to Haran to try to find a wife for Isaac. It was a dangerous journey. Eliezer took with him ten camels, several attendant servants and many valuable presents.

*(Create a camel hand-shadow on the wall.)*

For days and days they traveled, crossing valleys, hills and rivers and walking beside the great lonely desert.

*(Move the shadow-camel slowly across the wall.)*

Finally they came to Haran, and the tired camels knelt down near a well.

*(Let the camel's head droop.)*

The well was where everyone got their water. It was evening, and the women of the city were coming to fill their pitchers. Eliezer prayed that

God would send a young woman to the well who would be a good wife for Isaac. "O Lord," he prayed, "I will ask a young woman for a drink. If she is the one you want to be Isaac's wife, please let her give my camels water, too. By this sign I shall know she is the right woman."

While Eliezer was still praying, a beautiful young woman approached. Eliezer asked her for a drink. Although he was a stranger, she spoke kindly to him and said she would draw water for his camels also. Again and again she filled her pitcher and poured the water into the trough for the thirsty camels.

*(Raise the camel's head.)*

Eliezer knew God had answered his prayers. The camels had helped choose a wife. Her name was Rebekah. She and Isaac were married and Rebekah also had a great faith in God.

When we see a camel, we remember the story of Isaac and Rebekah.

## BIBLE VERSES AND ANIMAL HAND-SHADOWS

**To help your grandchild memorize a Bible verse, create an animal hand-shadow that relates to a particular Bible verse. Then let the child form the hand-shadow and say the verse. Here are some ideas:**

*"The Lord is my shepherd. I have everything I need"* (Psalm 23:1, ICB).

*"But those who wait for the Lord shall renew their strength, they shall mount up with wings like eagles"* (Isaiah 40:31, NRSV).

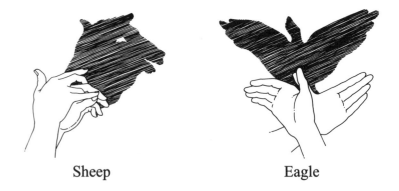

Sheep                    Eagle

**On the following page are a variety of simple-to-create hand-shadow creatures. (Note: The eagle above is also easy for even young children to create.) Here are some Bible verses you may want to share with your grandchildren as you "shadow play" together:**

*"For every wild animal of the forest is mine, the cattle on a thousand hills. I know all the birds of the air, and all that moves in the field is mine"* (Psalm 50:10–11, NRSV).

*"O Lord, how manifold are your works! In wisdom you have made them all; the earth is full of your creatures"* (Psalm 104:24, NRSV).

*"But ask the animals and they will teach you"* (Job 12:7, ICB).

*"I made the earth and everyone on it. I made all the animals on the earth. I did this with my great power and my strong arm"* (Jeremiah 27:5, ICB).

Elephant

**After you have tried these with your grandchildren, you may want to make up some others together. Experiment putting your fingers together one way or another. Use your imagination and see what pic-**

**tures you can make. For some extra fun, read the following verse to your grandchildren and then "load" shadow-animals into an imaginary ark.**

*"They had every kind of wild animal and tame animal. There was every kind of animal that crawls on the earth. Every kind of bird was there. They all came to Noah in the boat in groups of two. There was every creature that had the breath of life"* (Genesis 7:14–15, ICB).

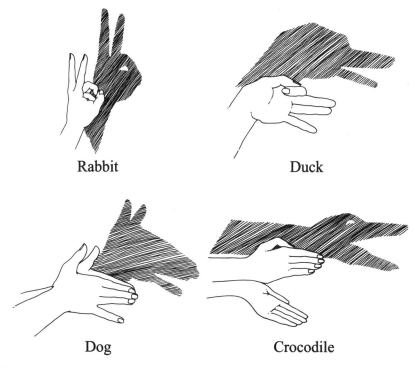

Rabbit                    Duck

Dog                      Crocodile

## Skit Bits

**D**ear Grandmother,

It's fun to act out stories as they are told. A child putting him/herself in another's shoes imagines, for a brief time, he really is that person or animal. It's fun to try to feel like another person, walk and talk like another person. These "skits and bits" are for one or more grandchildren of school age or for a grandchild and friends.

*"Remember your leaders. They taught God's message to you. Remember how they lived and died, and copy their faith. Jesus Christ is the same yesterday, today, and forever."*

—Hebrews 13:7–8, ICB

*"They should praise him with dancing. They should praise him with tambourines and harps."*

—Psalm 149:3, ICB

## EMOTION MARKERS

One of my favorite Bible stories is found in Mark 10:13–16, the story of Jesus and the children.

Help your grandchildren experience this story by using an idea from the ancient Kubaki theater of Japan. This type of theater dates back to 1586. Kubaki make-up is know as "Kumadori." The word *kumadori* means "pattern taking." The actor draws lines of color on his face that trace the pattern the blood takes as it flows through his veins in a characteristic emotion.

Read the story from the Bible to your grandchildren and talk about the emotions found in the story. **Ask:** "How were the disciples feeling?" **Say:** "Make a face to show how the disciples were feeling." **Let the children choose a *washable* marker in the color they think best expresses the emotion. Draw the lines on the child's face. Look at these in a mirror. Wash off the make-up. Ask:** "How were the children feeling?" **Say:** "Make a happy child's face." **Again choose a color and trace the lines on the child's face.**

If you have a number of grandchildren, leave the face make-up on one or more disciples and one or more happy-faced children. Then let the children act out the story.

You and your grandchildren might prefer to make your own face make-up. Here is a recipe:

Use an old muffin tin. In each cup of the tin mix 1 teaspoon cornstarch, 1/2 teaspoon water, 1/2 teaspoon cold cream and a couple of drops of food coloring (a different color for each cup). Stir each mixture well.

If the children do not wish to have their faces made up, use the colored markers to draw a face in the palm of each hand—an unhappy disciple's face in one palm and a happy child's face in the other. Let your grandchild tell you the story by opening the palms.

## A GAME OF CHANTS

Children love to play games and dance to rhythm. Create a game with your grandchild that helps him or her focus on the many creatures in God's world. Let the child pretend to be different animals.

If you can do simple chording on the piano (a four-beat measure in tonic [in C-major, C-E-G], two four-beat measures in dominant [G-B-D], another four-beat measure in tonic), it adds to the fun. If not, try clapping and chanting to this rhythm (the X's mark the beat):

"If you want to be a ____, here's your chance. Come on and do the ____ dance."

Try adding a drum for rhythm. A coffee can with a plastic lid makes a good drum. Beat it with your hand or a pencil.

A tambourine can be another homemade rhythm instrument. Make a tambourine by attaching things that rattle to the outer rim of a pie tin: metal buttons, tiny bells, pull tabs from soda cans. Punch a hole and attach the items with colored yarn. The more noisemakers, the better the sound.

Practice the rhythm with your grandchild.

Step 1: **The child decides what animal he would like to be—a tiger—for example.** Would this animal walk, run or skip? Experiment with the way a tiger would stalk.

Step 2: **Grandmother and child chant or sing** "If you want to be a tiger, here's your chance. Come on and do the tiger dance."

**The rhythm can be fast or slow, loud or soft as fits the animal.**

Step 3: **The child dances around like the animal chosen.**

Step 4: **After a while change to another animal. Ask the child:** "How would the movement be different?"

**Here are some suggestions:**

Be a kangaroo and use jumping movements. Hold your hands tightly to your body.

Be a wild horse and run in circles. Shake your mane.

Be an elephant and walk with slow, wide steps. Swing your head from side to side.

Be a caterpillar and crawl on your stomach.

Be a hummingbird and twirl in circles.

Step 5: **End with a short prayer thanking God for the many wonderful animals God has created.**

**The game can also be played with occupations, like a fireman, a pilot, etc.**

## ACTION VERSE

**Sometimes as grandmothers, we forget the great energy of young children. Outdoors or in a room with open space, read this poem to your grandchild. At the end of each verse, have him or her respond with the specified movement: hopping, galloping, skipping and jumping. What a great way to respond to God's gifts to us!**

*A blade from a bulb in the ground,*
*A circle of light shining 'round,*
*A grasshopper leaping so high,*
*Night stars filling the sky.*
*God made so much.*
*God doesn't stop.*
*When I think of these wonderful things,*
*I hop and I hop and I hop!*

*With a nudge God set the world a spinning.*
*When whirlwinds appeared God was grinning.*
*The rivers fast rushing,*
*Waterfalls gushing,*
*Power and energy,*
*Eagles in flight.*
*When I see all these wonderful things,*
*I gallop and gallop with all of my might!*

*A smile from the face of a friend,*
*A new baby's soft, dimpled hand,*
*Wiggly puppies licking my face,*

*I'm joining the wind in a race.*
*Good food to eat,*
*Cold milk on my lip.*
*When I think of these wonderful things,*
*I skip and I skip and I skip!*

*God's sun pops up in the morning,*
*Flower faces laugh at new day.*
*All God's creatures are singing.*
*It is early, early in May.*
*So much gladness,*
*So much to enjoy.*
*As I thank God for these wonderful things,*
*I jump and I jump and I jump for joy!*

## "PLAY-BACK" PLAY

**A tape recorder offers fun possibilities for you and your grandchildren. Physical closeness (because you need to be close to share one microphone) and cooperation are byproducts of this activity, and playing back always brings forth lots of giggles. The past is made present. One can be a creator and, two minutes later, a listener to that creation. Here are four ideas for using a tape recorder:**

*1. Play a "sounds game."*

*Thanksgiving with Grandmother*

**With your grandchild record all the sounds in the kitchen as you prepare for Thanksgiving dinner, and then let the rest of the family guess what the sounds are.**

**Here are some suggestions:**

(1) Water running
(2) Coffee perking
(3) Food sizzling in a pan
(4) Refrigerator door opening
(5) Toaster popping
(6) The cracking of eggs
(7) The sounds of beating eggs in a dish
(8) The pop of a drink can opening
(9) The whizz of an electric can opener
(10) The crunch of bread crumbs
(11) The bubbling of something boiling
(12) The tick-tock of a kitchen clock
(13) A door slamming
(14) The clink of dishes being set on the table

**Encourage the children to be creative in recording other sounds. As well as fun, this activity has the power to heighten sensory awareness.**

— — — — — — — — — — — — — — — —

*2. Use the tape recorder as a vehicle for sharing.*

**Pass the microphone around the entire family group asking each family member from the oldest to the youngest and any guests present that day to complete this sentence:**

**"I want to thank God for these things at Thanksgiving:_____**

**_____ ."**

**Play it back as a special Thanksgiving Day table blessing.**

*(Note: You could use this idea at any family gathering.)*

— — — — — — — — — — — — — — — —

*3. Use the tape recorder to make a Bible story come alive.*

**Before recording the following story on the tape recorder, you and your grandchildren need to experiment with ways to create sounds. At the beginning of the story, you will want to create the sounds of a peaceful pasture. How shall you make the sounds of a gently flowing stream? (Perhaps by dipping hands in a basin of water.) Can the children create animal**

sounds? (Sheep bleating, birds singing.) Using a soft blowing, can they sound like wind in trees? Wind in grasses? Encourage the children to use their voices, hands, feet, or props around them to explore different sound effects.

Tape these sounds and listen to them. Ask: "Are these the sounds we need for a peaceful feeling?"

Other sounds in this story are:

(1) Fire sounds of the burning bush. Crunching a piece of cellophane is a good fire sound.

(2) Footsteps. How shall Moses approach the bush? Swiftly? Slowly? You could use actual footsteps or hands hitting on a table.

(3) God's voice. To make it powerful, try amplifying the voice by speaking into an empty metal wastebasket. It will add a hollow echo-like sound to your voice.

(4) Do we want to add other "out-of-this-world" sounds? Lift the lid from a piano and stroke the strings with a feather or piece of tissue, or use a glissando.

When the children are pleased with the sounds, record the story. You or an older child may be the narrator.

### God Speaks to Moses from a Burning Bush

Though Moses was raised in a mighty Pharaoh's palace, he ran away and for many years lived the simple life of a shepherd. He was content to live in God's beautiful, peaceful outdoors. He learned much about pasture lands and watering places.

*(Create peaceful pasture sounds.)*

One day when Moses was out with his sheep he saw a strange sight—a flame of fire burst forth from a bush on a mountainside.

*(Fire sounds.)*

The flame kept burning, but the bush didn't burn up.

*(Fire sounds continue.)*

"What a strange sight," thought Moses. "I must take a closer look."

*(Sound of footsteps.)*

Then he heard a voice speaking from the bush.

*(God's voice, amplified)*: "TAKE OFF YOUR SHOES. YOU ARE STANDING ON HOLY GROUND."

Moses quickly took off his sandals.

(*Sound of shoes dropping.*)

(*God's voice, amplified*): "I AM THE GOD OF ABRAHAM, OF ISAAC, OF JACOB. I HAVE SEEN THE PAIN OF MY PEOPLE. I HAVE HEARD THEIR CRY. I KNOW THEIR SORROW. I WILL SEND YOU TO PHARAOH THE KING SO THAT YOU MAY BRING MY PEOPLE OUT OF EGYPT."

Poor Moses did not feel he was great enough to do such an important job. "If they ask, 'Who is this God?' What shall I say?"

(*God's voice, amplified*): "TELL THEM THAT MY NAME IS I AM, THE ONE WHO IS ALWAYS LIVING."

(*Out-of-this-world sounds.*)

— — — — — — — — — — — — — — —

4. *Use the tape recorder to tell the story above again.*

**After working on the Moses story, let each child tell the story again in his or her own words. From the youngest toddler to the oldest parent, have each go into a room alone and tell the story as he or she remembers it.**

**Then play back all the stories to see which parts were emphasized or omitted.**

## POCKET PUPPET

**It can be fun as a grandmother to have a special "story apron" with oversized pockets for times alone with your grandchild. Peeping out of the pocket can be the ear or tail of a furry hand puppet.**

**Invite your grandchild to feel (without looking) this mysterious creature. Feelings of fear, curiosity and excitement, and finally recognition emerge.**

**Pull out the puppet and let your grandchild name it. This little creature becomes an instant bridge to story or skit time.**

**The little furry friend can ask questions and find out things about your grandchild. It can introduce a story or listen as the child tells it a story. It can share the child's thoughts and prayers and sing along with him or her. Through this puppet your grandchild can be encouraged to explore and express feelings. Using the puppet, they can act out skits about things that make them sad or happy.**

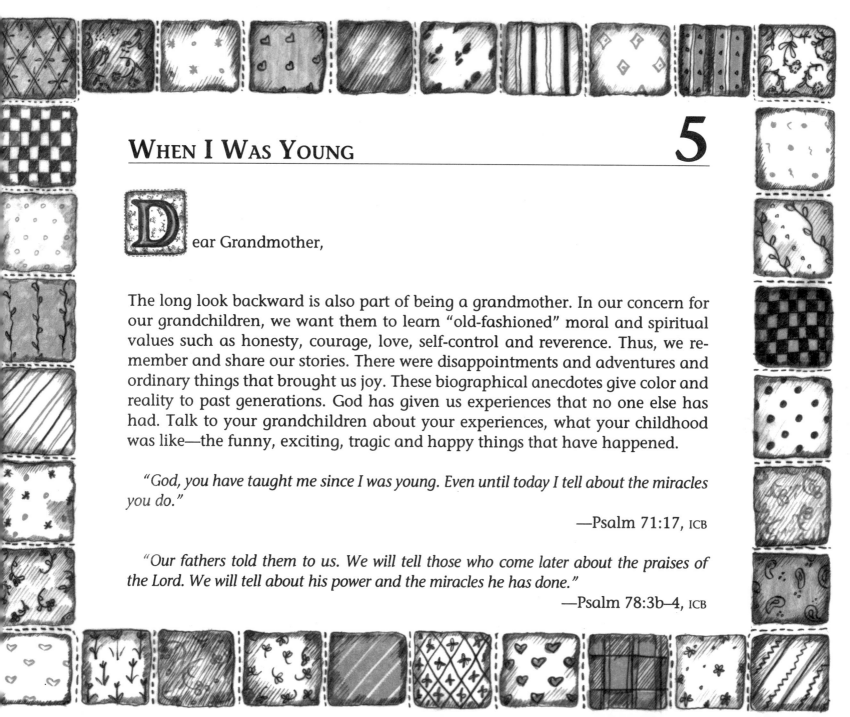

# WHEN I WAS YOUNG

**D**ear Grandmother,

The long look backward is also part of being a grandmother. In our concern for our grandchildren, we want them to learn "old-fashioned" moral and spiritual values such as honesty, courage, love, self-control and reverence. Thus, we remember and share our stories. There were disappointments and adventures and ordinary things that brought us joy. These biographical anecdotes give color and reality to past generations. God has given us experiences that no one else has had. Talk to your grandchildren about your experiences, what your childhood was like—the funny, exciting, tragic and happy things that have happened.

*"God, you have taught me since I was young. Even until today I tell about the miracles you do."*

—Psalm 71:17, ICB

*"Our fathers told them to us. We will tell those who come later about the praises of the Lord. We will tell about his power and the miracles he has done."*

—Psalm 78:3b–4, ICB

# I'll Tell You A Story

Words and music by Mary Lu Walker

*Refrain* I'll tell you a stor-y, tell you a stor-y. All a-bout the way it was when I was young. I'll sing you an old song. One I re-mem-ber, sing-ing in the old-en days.

*Verse 1.* I'll tell you of Moth-er when she was small, I'll tell you of Fa-ther be-fore he grew tall.

*Verse 2.* I'll tell you of hors-es, tell you of trains, I'll tell you of green fields and sum-mer rains.

**When my son was born in 1957 and my sister's child was born the same year, my mother wrote us the following letter. It has become a cherished heirloom in our family. Perhaps you would like to write your grandchild a letter of both laments and hurrahs.**

## A LETTER TO GIVE MY GRANDSONS
## BY
## LOUISE NEEL GATTIS

Dear Gloria and Judy,

Presenting your father and me with two grandsons makes a brimful, eventful year. Truly "our cup runneth over." My wish is that Paul and Neel may know something of the era in which your father and I grew up. In retrospect we often remember the lovely, but not always.

Hurrah, my grandsons won't be dosed with calomel and be drenched with castor oil. They won't have a flannel cloth soaked in coal oil and lard blister their chests. They won't have to endure long scratchy underwear from October to May or wear long black stockings and high-button shoes. Hurrah, they won't have to lime the privy, read by coal oil lamps, pick up corn cobs for kindling, eat sulphurated apples or shoo flies with peacock feathers.

Laments, though, because they will never know the excitement of hog-killing time, the magic words of "the thresher is coming," taste delectable cold clabber with crumbled-in cornbread or feel the cleanliness of homemade lye soap. And they probably won't ever know the tastiness of cold, fried shoulder meat, cooked in an iron skillet and served between two soft buttermilk biscuits. They won't ever use spoon holders or chew a slice of homemade bread spread with freshly churned butter. Too, they'll never know the sweetness of blackberry jam spooned from a gallon crock, or feel the breathless excitement of finding a new hen's nest in the barn loft.

Laments because they will miss the snugness of slumber with a nightcap on their heads and a hot wrapped brick at their feet, in a room around Eskimo temperature. Perhaps when Paul and Neel reach maturity all these things will be considered too simple for enjoyment. No doubt they will lament, "If only Grandma and Grandpa could have traveled at least to the moon."

These laments and hurrahs are the right of every generation.

---

**It is almost an understatement to say times certainly have changed since we**

**were young. Through the stories of our childhood, we can share with our grandchildren the unique victories and disappointments of days gone by. The following is one such story. Perhaps you have some "homespun" stories your own grandchildren will learn from and enjoy.**

## THE BLUE HORSE GLOVE

When Grandpa David was growing up in a small southwest Virginia mountain town, there were no Toys-R-Us or Kids Warehouse stores. And even if there had been, he would not have been able to purchase much with the money he made. He occasionally got 25¢ for mowing Mrs. Watson's rolling lawn with the rickety push mower and 5¢ a basket for raspberries picked from the brambles.

But there was a wonderful wish list available to elementary children in the 1940s: Blue Horse notebook paper! This staple of all grade-school children came with a special blue sheet enclosed. On this sheet were described all manner of wonderful toys, games and equipment. One item on this sheet was a baseball glove, and oh, how Grandpa wanted that baseball glove!

All you had to do was save blue sheets from the notebook paper until you had enough. One sheet came in each pack of paper.

David began saving—one sheet at a time. It takes a long time to use up a pack of notebook paper when you are ten years old. And, in a little mountain town in southwest Virginia, you didn't waste notebook paper. Notebook paper was for homework.

But slowly the pile of blue sheets grew. His brother helped. Friends, though usually saving for their own gifts, occasionally shared a sheet. Even his little sister was able to collect one or two.

Then one glorious day David had enough. He marched proudly to Mr. Palmer's General Store with a cardboard box full of Blue Horse sheets under his arm. His heart pounded as he thought of the gift that would soon be his.

Carefully Mr. Palmer took David's blue sheets and helped him fill out the information to accompany the sheets. A first-rate baseball glove of the finest quality was being ordered. To be sure that it fit his hand perfectly, there was even a place on the form to trace his hand. Proudly David plopped his right hand in the designated spot and Mr. Palmer traced an outline.

The request form and carefully folded blue sheets were dispatched. Then another waiting period began.

As David played baseball with the neighborhood children in the back field behind the big brick home, he dreamed of his baseball glove. What daring catches he would make! What flying leaps! What breathtaking swoops! Throughout the summer he played and dreamed and waited.

One crisp fall day, David was kicking the leaves along the sidewalk in front of Mr. Palmer's store when a voice called out:

"David, a package has arrived for you."

He hurried inside, ripped open the paper, and there it was—his long-awaited baseball glove. The fresh leather smell filled his nostrils. He carefully touched the shiny brown finish. It looked and smelled so new. Carefully he lifted it from the box to try it on and punch it soundly with the fist of his other hand, to begin to mold it to become his unique glove.

It was beautiful! It was magnificent! But something was wrong. Something was terribly wrong.

As he pantomimed catching a fly ball and hurling it to first base, David realized the problem. This was a right-hand glove. A good fielder puts his glove on his left hand so his right hand is free to throw the ball. When Mr. Palmer had traced his right hand, the company assumed he wanted a right-hand glove.

David tried for a while to catch with the new glove. Sometimes he put it on his left hand, but the thumb was always in a funny place. Sometimes he put it on his right hand and tried to throw with his left. But that didn't work either.

Finally Mr. Palmer agreed to send the glove back and ask for a left-hand one.

Neither David nor Mr. Palmer ever heard from the glove company again.

In these days of Consumer Rights, this story would have had a happier ending. But Grandpa David learned that disappointments are a part of every life, that both spontaneous joy and tears make up our days.

And when Grandpa David plays ball with you today and wears a glove that fits just right, he remembers the comfort and love of his family and friends when he was a little boy, feeling the pain of disappointment.

---

**Though trips to exotic locations can bring forth equally exotic tales, my mother here shows us how an everyday activity became quite exciting! Recall for your grandchildren "the everyday" of your youth (it is now very probably "the unusual"!)**

## GRANDMA'S SAFARI
## BY LOUISE NEEL GATTIS

I am a member of that inclusive breed who exclaim, most ungrandma-ish, "I'm exhausted! My grandchildren have been visiting me. What a joy and what a relief to see them leave."

What is wrong with the grandmothers of this era? They deplete themselves entertaining the grandchildren, rushing them to swimming pools, theme parks, and keeping a good supply of videos.

My grandmother didn't expend half the energy we moderns do today. Yet I have only to open the memory doors of childhood and recall that even Grandma's daily tasks took on an aura of excitement. My grandmother could make a simple chore, like going to the henhouse, as exciting as a safari in Africa.

In the spring, when the maternal instinct reached its peak, she often had as many as ten hens setting. A setting hen can present a terrifying picture with ruffled feathers, sharp beaks and unlidded eyes. With Daniel-like bravery she would reach under those squawky, aspiring mothers and remove the fresh eggs.

I liked just standing in the doorway holding the wicker egg basket as Grandma went from hen to hen. But when she called Fido and Shep to go with us down the path to the henhouse, both the dogs and I tingled because we knew instinctively something big was about to happen.

This time I stood just outside the door while Grandma stepped calmly over the sill and with the dexterity of a circus performer reached under the silent setting hen and agilely pulled out, by the tail, a six-foot chicken snake whose humped body was evidence of an egg thief.

She threw it to the eager, barking dogs, who gleefully shook the snake into shreds. Going on to the next nest, she would give the same barehand performance because snakes usually worked in pairs.

The same grandma would return from this event, wash her hands, remove her split bonnet, tie a clean white apron around her waist and say, "Come, Mary Louise, it is time for your catechism lesson."

I don't believe she was ever exhausted by my visit, and I know I was never bored.

———

**A family name is something special, something to be proud of. Younger children like to say names, and older children are interested in where names came from. Share with your grandchild all you know about your name. Is anyone in your family a namesake (one named for another)? Share the following action story about a namesake. Read the story and pantomime the action.**

## GRAHAM'S RABBITS

Once there was a little boy named Graham who had a problem. His problem was rabbits. (*Children hop around, acting like rabbits.*) Graham loved his pet rabbits very dearly (*pat them on head*), but he was very poor and had no money to buy food for them. (*Graham turns pockets inside out.*) At first he went out every day and picked grass for them to eat. (*Pantomime action: bend over, pick grass, feed rabbits.*) This made the rabbits very happy. (*Rabbits hop all around.*) But Graham lived in a city apartment, and soon all the grass in his small yard was gone. Besides, this wasn't a very good diet for growing rabbits.

Next Graham walked and walked until he found a vacant lot with grass. (*Pantomime walking.*) He called his rabbits and they ate happily. (*Rabbits pantomime eating.*) But there were cars whizzing by and cats lurking near, and Graham decided this was just too dangerous. Once one of his rabbits almost got hit by a car. (*Graham pantomimes narrowly saving rabbit.*) Once a cat almost had a rabbit for dinner. (*Graham pantomimes narrowly saving rabbit.*)

Graham took all his rabbits back to his apartment. (*Pantomime action.*) What was Graham to do? (*Graham pantomimes worry.*) He loved his rabbits too much to give them away (*Graham pets rabbits*), but he couldn't see them starve to death. Then Graham had an idea! He ran to the phone and called his friends and asked them to come over. (*Graham pantomimes calling.*)

"I have an important announcement to make!" Graham said. "I have just named my rabbits. As you can see, I have named each rabbit for one of my special friends." (*Children smile, pantomiming approval.*)

The children were very honored and happy. "I don't have quite enough food for this rabbit," Graham said, sadly patting his first rabbit. (*Pantomime action.*) "What, not enough food for my namesake?" said his friend. "Why, I will see that he gets enough food." (*Friend takes food from pocket and feeds his rabbit.*) "And I'll feed mine." "Me too," said each of his other friends. (*Friends pantomime action.*)

So all of the rabbits had plenty to eat and were happy and playful (*rabbits hop around*), all of the friends were proud of their namesakes (*friends pantomime pride*) and Graham kept his rabbits and his friends.

We have been called the children of God. We, too, like the rabbits, are namesakes and will not be forsaken.

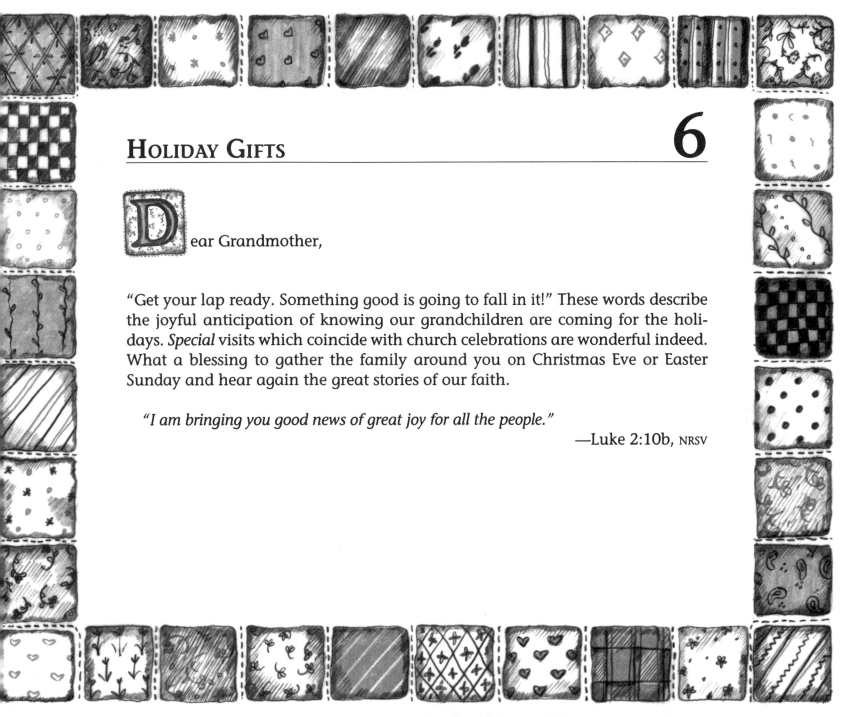

## HOLIDAY GIFTS

Dear Grandmother,

"Get your lap ready. Something good is going to fall in it!" These words describe the joyful anticipation of knowing our grandchildren are coming for the holidays. *Special* visits which coincide with church celebrations are wonderful indeed. What a blessing to gather the family around you on Christmas Eve or Easter Sunday and hear again the great stories of our faith.

*"I am bringing you good news of great joy for all the people."*

—Luke 2:10b, NRSV

In this loud, commercialized, neon-lit, mall-packed Christmas season, what gifts do I want to give to my grandchildren?

- **Christmas Carols to Brighten Their Way**
- **A "Window" to Christmas**
- **A Story to Make Them Laugh**
- **Stories to Stretch Their Imagination**
- **A Fun Game to Play**
- **Something Homemade . . .**

## CHRISTMAS CAROLS TO BRIGHTEN THEIR WAY

Songs and dances always add to a celebrative atmosphere.

Is *"Jingle Bells"* the only Christmas song your grandchildren know? Or *"Frosty the Snowman"* or *"Rudolph the Red-nosed Reindeer"*?

Sing the shepherd songs, too.

Begin saving material for a shepherd's box. Save old bathrobes, towels or dish towels, tie-backs from draperies, old sashes. There may even be an old stuffed-toy lamb or a tree branch shaped like a shepherd's crook. Let the grandchildren play dress-up.

Then all gather around the piano and sing the shepherd carols. Here are a few:

*"It Came Upon a Midnight Clear"*
*"O Little Town of Bethlehem"*
*"Silent Night"*
*"While Shepherds Watched Their Flocks by Night"*
*"The First Noel"*

A grandchild may be able to play a recorder or flute. These go well with the shepherd carols.

And since they are all dressed up, the grandchildren might like to have a "Shepherds Going to Bethlehem Parade" around the house—around the neighborhood—down the street. Then back to Grandma's house for hot chocolate and cookies.

Here is a new way to tell toddlers a beautiful old story . . .

## WINDOWS TO CHRISTMAS

I will tell you a Christmas story, but you must give me windows to look through so that I can look far into the past. Can you make a window like this?

(*Child puts hands on hips. Grandmother peeps through.*)

Yes, that is good. I can see far, far away. I see a little village. It's the village of Bethlehem, lying along the slope and on the top of a gray hill. Beyond is a range of higher hills. Oh yes, I see more. There are brooks filled with water, but sometimes they are only dry beds of stone. There are lots of grey stones peeping through the soil. There are mighty cedar trees stretching out their sweeping branches. There are oak trees sturdy and rich with dark leaves. Listen. The wind is blowing over the plains. Along the slopes I see the shiny leaves of grapevines. Twisted, gnarled olive trees are there. Now I see low houses, many of mud and sunburned brick. Cattle are very near the houses. They are stamping their feet and crunching their food. I can just make out a group of buildings clustered together around a courtyard. It's an inn of some sort for travelers. I will need to look through another window to see it better.

Can you make a window like this?

(*Child raises arms above head, touching hands, to create a window. Grandmother looks through.*)

Yes, that's good. Now I see clearly. Yes, it's a place where travelers come. Smoke is rising from campfires. Food is cooking. From there you can see other travelers coming up to the village, some on donkeys, some on horses, some on foot. Tonight the inn is all filled up. Every area surrounding the courtyard is filled with people. There is not an inch more space for the other travelers who continue to come. Yet, I think there is shelter to be had. It looks like there are caves scooped out of the soft chalk rocks. This must be the place where horses and donkeys and oxen are kept. I will need another window to see more clearly. Can you make a window like this?

(*Child places thumb and forefinger together, creating a small window. Grandmother peeps through.*)

That's very good. Now I see something wonderful. A man and a young woman are in this cave-stable, and a child has been born to Mary, the mother. It is the baby Jesus. Though they are travelers far away from their home, there seem to be friends there in this lonely place. I see shepherds kneeling by the manger where the baby lies. I smell fragrant hay. There are animals—great, gentle oxen; friendly, funny donkeys; soft, cuddly lambs. The animals nod with glad eyes. There is a glow, a beautiful shining in this place. Through your tiny window I can just make out a bright, bright star.

The picture is fading now.

It happened long, long ago, but we still remember. It is a very important story in our lives.

## A STORY TO MAKE THEM LAUGH

**If you have four or more grandchildren use only the children in this action story. If less, enlist the parents. Read this at a good fast pace—it is funnier that way.**

*King Herod and the Wise Men*

Child 1:   Every time he or she hears THIS—raise the right hand and say "Right on!"

Child 2:   Every time he or she hears THAT—raise the left hand and say "Watch out!"

Child 3:   Every time he or she hears KING HEROD—raise both hands and say "Oh my!"

Child 4:   Every time he or she hears BABY JESUS—say "Ahhhh."

THIS (*Right on!*) is the story about the birth of JESUS (*Ahhhh*) and how the wicked KING HEROD (*Oh my!*) tried to have him killed.

Now on THAT (*Watch out!*) night the chief priests and the scribes told KING HEROD (*Oh my!*) that a new ruler of the people would be born in Bethlehem.

THIS (*Right on!*) new ruler was of course, BABY JESUS (*Ahhhh*). THAT (*Watch out!*) caused KING HEROD (*Oh my!*) to become anxious and worried.

"How can I get rid of THAT (*Watch out!*) child?" KING HEROD (*Oh my!*) asked. "Aha! I think I have a plan THAT (*Watch out!*) will do just THAT (*Watch out!*)."

"Question those wise men from the east," KING HEROD (*Oh my!*) ordered. "THAT (*Watch out!*) should do it. They know where THAT (*Watch out!*) child is to be found."

And THIS (*Right on!*) is what KING HEROD (*Oh my!*) tried to do. But THAT (*Watch out!*) plan did not work at all. The wise men said, "We only know to follow THIS (*Right on!*) star."

"Hmmm," KING HEROD (*Oh my!*) said. "THAT (*Watch out!*) is not enough to go on. My scholars tell me BABY JESUS (*Ahhhh*) is to be born in THAT (*Watch out!*) little town of Bethlehem."

"THIS (*Right on!*) is a good place to start looking," the wise men thought, and they rode off in THIS (*Right on!*) direction.

"THAT (*Watch out!*) should do it," KING HEROD (*Oh my!*) said. "I'll let them do the searching for BABY JESUS (*Ahhhh*), and I'll send my soldiers to THAT (*Watch out!*) place when they have found him and have him killed."

The wise men looked up and saw the guiding star. "THIS (*Right on!*) is the way to Bethlehem and to the BABY JESUS (*Ahhhh*)," they said.

Then THIS (*Right on!*) star came to rest over a stable in Bethlehem and there the wise men found BABY JESUS (*Ahhhh*) and they fell down and worshiped Him.

But THIS (*Right on!*) is not the end of the story. Would they go back and report to KING HEROD (*Oh my!*)? Is THAT (*Watch out!*) what the wise men should do?

Perhaps they would have done just THAT (*Watch out!*). But instead, THIS (*Right on!*) is what happened: An angel appeared to the wise men in a dream and said, "THIS (*Right on!*) is what you must do. Do not take THAT (*Watch out!*) road back to KING HEROD (*Oh my!*), but go back home another way—THIS (*Right on!*) way." And the angel pointed in the opposite direction.

The wise men followed the advise of THIS (*Right on!*) dream. They left for their own country. And the BABY JESUS (*Ahhhh*) was saved.

And THIS (*Right on!*) is the story of THAT (*Watch out!*) wicked KING HEROD (*Oh my!*) and the birth of BABY JESUS (*Ahhhh*).

## STORIES TO STRETCH THE IMAGINATION

**As we continue to tell the Christmas stories, we challenge our grandchildren to try to imagine what it really would have been like to have been in Bethlehem on that first Christmas so long ago. What would we have seen? What would we have heard?**

**Bring the senses into play for some new experiences of the traditional stories . . .**

*Listen to the Angels*

**Most of us grandmothers have accumulated bells of some sort: glass dinner bells, small brass bells given as gifts long ago, maybe even silver bells. With the grandchildren, gather up all these bells—one for each grandchild. Or invite each grandchild to bring a special bell with him or her when they come to visit.**

**Explain that no one knows what angels sound like but that they must have very beautiful voices—maybe like a bell.**

**Read Luke 2:8–15 (ICB). Ask the grandchildren to listen carefully and ring their bells every time they hear the word ANGEL:**

*"That night, some shepherds were in the fields nearby watching their sheep. An ANGEL of the Lord stood before them. The glory of the Lord was shining around them, and suddenly they became very frightened. The ANGEL said to them, 'Don't be afraid, because I am bringing you some good news. It will be a joy to all the people. Today your Savior was born in David's town. He is Christ, the Lord. This is how you will know him: You will find a baby wrapped in cloths*
*and lying in a feeding box.' Then a very large group of ANGELS from heaven joined the first ANGEL. All the ANGELS were praising God, saying: 'Give glory to God in heaven, and on earth let there be peace to the people who please God.' Then the ANGELS left the shepherds and went back to heaven."*

*Walk with the Wise Men*

**You will need four large sturdy trays. Let the children help you gather supplies for these trays. Tray 1: moss and leaves. Tray 2: smooth rocks and stones. Tray 3: sand. Tray 4: water. Or use your imagination and the children's imagination and add to the trays whatever you like that will be good objects to feel with your feet.**

**Place the four trays on the floor—a porch is a good place. The children take off their shoes and socks. As you read the story of the wise men from Matthew 1:18–2:12 (or, even better, tell it in your own words), the children walk through these four trays. Tell the children to use the feel of the different objects on their feet to help them understand the long, hard journey of the wise men.**

**Afterward clean the children's feet and talk with them about the experience.**

*The Christmas Aromas*

**Gather four containers of smells: a piney, outdoor smell; straw; a floral smell; a spicy smell or perfume.**

**Read Luke 2:8 (ICB)—***"That night, some shepherds were in the fields nearby watching their sheep."* **Let the grandchildren smell the piney outdoor smells. Say: "Let this smell help you imagine the shepherds in the fields."**

**Read Luke 2:16 (NRSV)—***"So they went with haste and found Mary and Joseph, and the child lying in the manger."* **Let your grandchildren smell the straw and the floral smell. Ask: "Does this help you imagine how the manger must have been and how fresh a newborn baby smells?"**

**Read Matthew 2:1, 2 (ICB)—***"Jesus was born in the town of Bethlehem in Judea during the time when Herod was king. After Jesus was born, some wise men from the east came to Jerusalem. They asked, 'Where is the baby who was born to be the king of the Jews? We saw his star in the east. We came to worship him.'"* **Explain that in the east where the wise men came from there were exotic, spicy smells. Let the grandchildren smell the spice or perfume. Say: "Let the smell help you imagine the wise men."**

**(Note: Gather evergreens for your house and encourage your grandchildren to sniff and smell. We often associate happy times with aromas. Baking cookies and Christmas cakes are also wonderful smells!)**

## A FUN GAME TO PLAY

**Playing games with cousins who have also come to visit grandmother can be a fun occasion at Christmas. Some of the old-time games like "Hide and Seek" and "Kick the Can" are brand new and exciting to modern grandchildren. Here's a fun one to try . . .**

*A Shepherd Game*

**The more grandchildren the better for this old-time game, but it can be played with only two children plus Grandmother. Decide upon goal area and keep one grandchild (shepherd) at this area while the other grandchild (sheep) hides. When**

the sheep is hidden, Grandmother says "Okay" and the other grandchild (shepherd) goes looking. If the shepherd spies the sheep, the shepherd cries "Run Sheep Run" and they both race back to the goal, each trying to get there first. Even if the shepherd has not yet discovered the sheep, Grandmother can call "Run Sheep Run" if she feels the shepherd is far enough away for the sheep to reach the goal safely.

Playing with only two grandchildren works fine if the children are young and they take turns being shepherd and sheep. If you have many grandchildren and friends, then form two teams—a shepherd team and a sheep team. When the first shepherd finds the first sheep and calls "Run Sheep Run," all the team members race for the goal. Grandmother can sit back and watch this time.

## SOMETHING HOMEMADE

Can you sew or knit? Is painting your gift, or crafts? Perhaps there is a special skill,

such as paper-cutting or lace-making, which has been passed down in your family. Maybe you can make up original songs or poems. When we make something special for our grandchildren, the gift itself is only a part of the joy. We have the pleasure of thinking about the grandchild as we create, as we choose colors or shapes just for him or her, as we decide which image or object would delight this special child.

The children have the pleasure of knowing they have something unique—something made just for them. When something is handmade, there is no other one in the world exactly like it.

Give your grandchildren something homemade and encourage them to create something for you. One grandmother wrote the following song for her grandson . . .

# Patrick's Red Sweater

**Words and music by Mary Lu Walker**

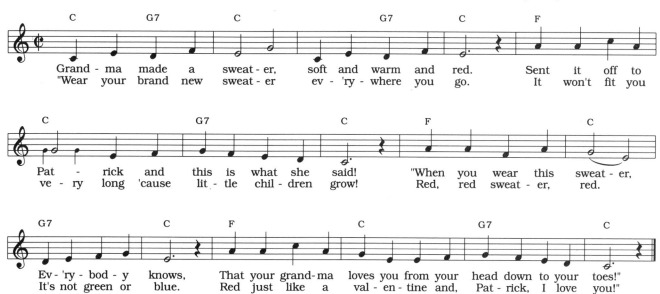

Grand - ma made a sweat - er, soft and warm and red. Sent it off to
"Wear your brand new sweat - er ev - 'ry - where you go. It won't fit you

Pat - rick and this is what she said! "When you wear this sweat - er,
ve - ry long 'cause lit - tle chil - dren grow! Red, red sweat - er, red.

Ev - 'ry - bod - y knows, That your grand - ma loves you from your head down to your toes!"
It's not green or blue. Red just like a val - en - tine and, Pat - rick, I love you!"

And what would I wish for my grand-children on Easter, our greatest of all church celebrations?

I'd like them to know:

- **Our Biblical Easter Story**
- **Easter Is a Time for Thinking of Others and Sharing**
- **Manners Make the Easter Feast Pleasant for All**
- **Even Easter Eggs Can Carry Important Messages**

## THE EASTER STORY

How can we tell the familiar story so that ears will hear it anew? Try accompanying the story of Easter morning with paper sounds. Cut strips of paper from tissue sheets from a whole spectrum of colors. Let the children experiment with the sounds that paper can make, and as you read aloud the following scripture from Matthew 28 (icb), have the children make accompanying sounds.

"The day after the Sabbath day was the first day of the week. At dawn on the first day, Mary Magdalene and another woman named Mary went to look at the tomb." (*Crunch the paper very slowly. Listen to the sound.*)

"At that time there was a strong earthquake. An angel of the Lord came down from heaven. The angel went to the tomb and rolled the stone away from the entrance. Then he sat on the stone." (*Rip a sheet of paper dramatically.*) "He was shining as bright as lightning. His clothes were white as snow. The soldiers guarding the tomb were very frightened and then became like dead men." (*Shake the paper.*)

"The angel said to the women, 'Don't be afraid. I know that you are looking for Jesus, the one who was killed on the cross. But he is not here. He has risen from death as he said he would.

Come and see the place where his body was. And go quickly and tell his followers. . . .'

"The women left the tomb quickly. They were afraid, but they were also very happy. They ran to tell Jesus' followers what had happened." (*Crunch the paper quickly.*) "Suddenly, Jesus met them and said, 'Greetings.' The women came up to Jesus, took hold of his feet, and worshiped him." (*Whirl the colored strips of paper around your head joyfully.*)

**Sing "Christ the Lord Is Risen Today." Even the youngest can join in the allelujahs.**

## AN OFFERING FOR OTHERS

**When grandchildren come to visit for Easter, we can teach them to use money as a way of thinking of others and expressing thankfulness and compassion. Tell this story:**

When Jesus was sharing His last supper with His friends, He wanted to let them know more about how God wants us to live. So He rose from the table, got a towel and a basin of water, and began to wash His disciples' feet.

The disciples were puzzled. They had washed the dust from their feet before coming into the room. But Jesus was saying, "We must do what we can to help others. It can be simple things. We can all help."

**Talk about ways your grandchildren can help. Say:** "Since we can't be everywhere, helping everyone, sometimes we can give money. Let's start a helping bank."

**Use a bank that you have, or create one from a milk carton. Get a large pile of pennies if your grandchildren are preschoolers. If they are older, they can use their own money from their allowance.**

**You may wish to focus the act of giving money like this:**

1. Ask the children to remember how Jesus rode into Jerusalem on a donkey. Say: "In many parts of the world, a car is a great luxury." Let the children put twenty-five pennies into the bank for every car their family owns.

2. Explain that many children do not have a home. Perhaps you can give a personal example from your area. Let the children count the doors in your (or their) house and put two cents in the bank for every door.

3. In some places in the world, children don't have fresh water to drink. Say: "Put in ten cents for every good drink of water you have had today."

4. In some places children do not have enough to eat. Say: "Put one cent in the bank for every can of food in this house."

5. Talk to the children about those who do not have warm clothes. Let the children put five cents in the bank for each coat or sweater he or she owns.

6. Think about those who are sick. Say: "Put twenty-five pennies in the bank if you haven't been sick in the last month."

**Let the children suggest other persons or situations that could use their money to help. Then thank God together in prayer for all these blessings: transportation, shelter, fresh water, plentiful food, warm clothing and good health.**

**The children can take the bank with their special helping money to their Sunday School class as an offering on Easter morning.**

**After attending the Easter service together, how special it is to have the family for Easter dinner, everyone together at the table, even the babies in highchairs.**

**Here are some ways to make it more pleasant . . .**

## MANNERS MUSIC

**Sometime before the meal play a game with the very young grandchildren to teach table manners.**

**Seated on the floor, tell the children that five friends are coming to teach them table manners. Hold up your hand with the five fingers extended.**

"Here they are. First is Tommy Thumb." (*Wiggle your thumb and encourage the children to do the same.*) "Tommy has lots of toys, but he knows not to bring the toys to the table. Listen to what he says."

(*Sing these words and melody*):

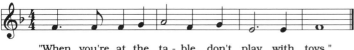

"When you're at the ta-ble, don't play with toys."

(*Ask the children to sing with you, wiggling their thumbs.*)

"Now here is Sally Second-Finger." (*Hold up your second finger.*) "Sally sits very straight at the table, never tilting her chair or trying to climb down. Listen to what Sally says." (*Using the same melody, sing the following.*)

"When you're at the ta-ble, stay in your chair."

(*Now ask the children to sing along with you.*)

"Here comes Thelma Third-Finger. Now Thelma always says 'Please' when she wants something at the table. 'May I please have some bread?' 'Will you please pass the salt?' Listen to Thelma," (*Sing the following.*)

"When you're at the ta-ble, al-ways say 'Please'."

(*The children sing after you.*)

"Freddy Fourth-Finger use to have trouble at the table." (*Hold up the fourth finger.*) "He would grab and spill and drop things, but now he has manners. Listen to what he says." (*Sing the following.*)

"When you're at the ta - ble, nev - er reach and grab."

(*The children sing after you.*)

"Here comes Lester Little-Finger. Hi, Lester! Lester knows special words to say when he has finished eating." (*Sing the following.*)

"When the meal is ov - er, say, 'May I be ex - cused?'"

(*The children sing after you.*)

"Can we remember the manners our five friends have taught us?":

> Don't play with toys.
> Stay in your chair.
> Always say "Please."
> Never reach or grab.
> Say: "May I be excused?"

### BIBLE VERSE EGGS

**When we give our grandchildren memory verses from the Bible, we are giving them valuable treasures. Take some familiar Bible verses such as those suggested below. Type or print them on strips**

**of paper. Then cut the words apart and put the pieces in a plastic Easter egg. The child takes apart the egg and solves the Bible verse puzzle. All of the following verses are from the *International Children's Bible*.**

*"The Lord gives me strength and makes me sing"* (Exodus 15:2a).

*"Thank the Lord because he is good"* (1 Chronicles 16:34a).

*"First I want to say that I thank my God through Jesus Christ for all of you"* (Romans 1:8a).

*"Give thanks whatever happens"* (1 Thessalonians 5:18a).

*"God is our protection and our strength"* (Psalm 46:1a).

*"God, have mercy on us and bless us"* (Psalm 67:1a).

*"Sing for joy to God, our strength"* (Psalm 81:1).

*"Serve the Lord with joy"* (Psalm 100:2a).

*"Come near to God, and God will come near to you"* (James 4:8a).

Dear Grandmother,

And finally there are all the little experiences that make your grandmothering unique. Here are a few hints (and even some food favorites) I have tried and some from friends. I call them "Grandmother Grace Notes" in honor of those little ornaments in music that add an extra sparkle. Though most all hints can be adapted to both in-town and out-of-town grandmothering, I have starred (*) those hints *especially* for out-of-town grandmothers.

*"But plans succeed when you get advice from many others."*

—Proverbs 15:22b, ICB

*"Grandchildren are the reward of old people."*

—Proverbs 17:6a, ICB

## 23 GRACE NOTES

*1. If your grandchild lives out of town, send him or her postcards. You can buy books of postcards with wonderful themes—teddy bears, Peter Rabbit, etc. Or send picture postcards from your hometown or a local museum. Little children love getting their own mail. The message need not be elaborate. You could say, "How many birds do you see in this picture?" or, "I walked by this house today" or, "When I saw this at the museum, I thought of you."

2. Attend garage sales and look for things your grandchild could play "dress-up" with. Recently I found a fireman's hat and a fur muff.

*3. I learned this one from my daughter-in-law. Make the child his or her own photo album. Put in pictures of Grandmother and Grandfather, pictures of all the pets and especially pictures of the grandchild. A good way to have pictures on hand is to have a second set printed each time you have film developed. (Many photo places offer extra prints either free or at a significant discount.) As soon as the child begins to recognize faces, let him or her play with the album. If it gets torn up, that's okay, too.

4. I had a box of art prints from an Art Appreciation class I had taken in college. It had been gathering dust for years. Sarah Neel (one of my granddaughters) loved having these for her own "books," and hopefully she is absorbing an appreciation of good art. The same is true of music. We can expose our grandchildren to beauty at an early age.

5. Most families have a special vocabulary, words that have grown out of specific situations and often make sense only to family members. Share these with your grandchild. In our family we have *Klokomoko!* for panicky situations and *sandjank* for the special back rub Grandmother Lou gives.

*6. Begin a collection of something for your grandchild, and bring something new for it on each visit or each special occasion or from each trip you take. It could be a silver spoon or a thimble or a pennant or a postcard or a special little ceramic animal.

*7. Plant a special tree in the yard named for your grandchild and send him or her pictures as the tree grows. Flowering fruit trees are especially nice.

8. Bring little memories back from your vacation— sea shells or black sand or tiny pebbles.

9. Give your grandchild a flowering plant for his or her special care. It could be a cutting from one of yours.

*10. Keep a guest book. Jot down or have older grandchildren jot down a few memories of each visit. Memories slip away so fast.

*11. Recycle your own children's toys, and have them on hand when the grandchildren come for a visit. Put new suspenders on the old teddy bear, restuff the well-worn monkey, buy or make new dresses for the old babydoll. Keep a special chest or box of these toys ready for a grandchild's visit and exploration.

*12. Wondering what to do when the grandchildren come for a visit? Remember that doing is the point of life for children. They can talk. They can sing. They can fantasize. They can play roles. They can draw. They can dance. They can paste. They can discuss. They can write. They can MOVE! Space, freedom and acceptance can make a lively, active, creative visit possible. Check out the zoos. One grandmother I know takes her grandchildren to count the cats at Mrs. Hoover's house. (They have seen as many as 36!) Check out the wading creeks and streams. Go for walks and collect things—rocks, feathers, leaves. Or count things—mailboxes and flags and squares on the sidewalk. Or find everything that is red. Bring stale bread and go feed the ducks, or the fish, or the pigeons.

*13. Celebrate birthdays. One grandmother I know celebrates birthdays whenever her grandchildren come for a visit. If anyone in the family has had a birthday since the last time they were all together, out comes the birthday cake and ice cream. Up go the balloons and banners. There is one cake, but presents for all.

*14. A grandmother I know went to visit her grandson and took him a small present in a yellow bag. The next visit he asked if she had brought a yellow bag. Now she always takes him something in a yellow bag.

15. If you are a grandmother who can sew, make a tooth fairy pillow for your grandchild.

*16. Children love traditions. A special food can be served every time a grandchild comes to visit. Perhaps one kind of cookie. Sarah Neel always wants Chinese food for her birthday dinner.

17. Celebrate whenever you can. When Grandpa David received a special award, the whole family made a big deal out of it. Using a bright red plastic tablecloth, we created a robe and bought a paper crown. He was "King for the Day." Didn't the father celebrate the return of the Prodigal Son by bringing out a special robe? Sarah Neel and Laura (our granddaughters) decorated a large sheet of mural paper and taped it to the front door. We all sang and danced for the "king."

18. Have you tried peanut butter playdough? It is a real grandmother treat! Here is the recipe: Mix one part honey with three or four parts smooth peanut butter. Blend well. Then gradually add powdered milk until it is the consistency of playdough. Give your grandchild a ball of this for creating and nibbling.

*19. Keep a circle of love going through your family if your family is scattered. Send a thought on a full sheet of paper to your adult child. This child adds his current good news or ideas answering: "What are the ideas that are exciting you now? What's the best news you know right now?" Then he or she sends it on to a brother or sister and then on to each grandchild. This is a way for the entire family to keep in touch. And it doesn't take a lot of time.

20. Many of us have warm thoughts about times spent with grandparents. They left an indelible mark on our memory because of some incident or ritual or place that was really rather ordinary but became

extraordinary to us—a feather bed, a warm quilt, a loud ticking clock. Create warm memories for your grandchild by designating special spots in your home where a child is free to do what a child loves to do. For example:

- A rolling place. Children love to roll on the floor, in grass, wherever.
- A magpie corner. Children love to accumulate, to put things in piles, to collect.
- A swinging place. A tire swing on a tree or a nearby playground will do.
- A secret place. A place where a child can hide. Let the child pick this.

We learn so much about trusting faith from the little ones. When things would begin to get frantic for little Laura, she would come and hold her hands up, asking to be held and cuddled. Then she would be fine and toddle on her way again. If we could only come to God this way in prayer—when our world gets frantic, just lift up our arms to be held and then, strengthened, go on our way again.

21. Grandmother can make writing thank-you notes fun for her grandchild. These thank-you notes can be created at a very early age if you say to the child: "This person was thinking about you and brought you this gift. Think about the gift and draw something so the person will know you liked it." Resist the temptation to tell the child what to draw.

22. The many free things that become throw-away in our culture can create moments of delight for your grandchild—the little cars in cereal boxes, the little jellies in restaurants, the little soaps and other free samples from hotels, the perfume page from ladies' magazines, just pretty pictures that say: "Hi! I'm thinking about you."

*23. One of the things out-of-town grandmothers miss is the day-to-day living with the child. Sometimes when grandchildren come for a quick visit, we see only their best (or worst!) behavior. But what is a child's day-to-day personality like? Here's an idea to try: Make a week-long calendar of boxes like the one on the following page (or you may copy this one), and send one or more calendars to your grandchild with a note. In the note, urge the child to share with you how he or she is feeling each day by drawing his or her own "face" in the appropriate block. I have also provided some examples of "feeling faces" you can copy and send to the child as ideas. Be sure to tell him or her that it's okay to draw more than one face on a particular day's block—sometimes our days turn upside-down! Assure your grandchild that it is all right to have all kinds of feelings and that he or she can always share them with you. Ask the child to mail you a completed calendar at the end of each week. (You might want to provide self-addressed and stamped envelopes in your original calendar package.) This "Calendar of Feelings" is a great way to keep in touch with your grandchild on a daily basis and encourage the freedom to express emotions. Note: You can add to the child's anticipation by exchanging with him or her a calendar of your own feelings.

| SUNDAY | MONDAY | TUESDAY | WEDNESDAY | THURSDAY | FRIDAY | SATURDAY |
|--------|--------|---------|-----------|----------|--------|----------|
|        |        |         |           |          |        |          |

HAPPY   JUST OKAY   SLEEPY   SAD   ANGRY

## FOOD FUN

### Animal Pancakes

When the generations gather together for breakfast, create animal pancakes. Make your favorite pancake recipe or use a packaged mix, making your mixture a little thicker than usual.

Pour the mix, in animal shapes, into a sizzling pan. You might begin with a Mickey Mouse profile: a large drop for the head and two small drops for ears. To add to the "animation," make faces on the cooked pancakes using raisins, cherries, marshmallows, red hots or other candies.

A long, oblong drop for a body, a little drop for a head, small dribbles for feet and tail can be a cat or a dog. Let your grandchild decide which it is.

The fun of this activity is that the shapes are hard to control. A planned dog can turn out to be a wonderful giraffe when the head elongates in cooking. An elephant may appear when a long trunk suddenly develops from a extra dribble.

Sometimes it takes imagination to see it, but children have the gift of seeing the world with fresh eyes and making delightful connections.

Try a rabbit with a round head and two long ears. My daughter-in-law has perfected the art of making a heart pancake, and this is a good one to end with.

## Popcorn

Popcorn is another fun food to share with the generations. It entices us by using all our senses. We smell it and hear it as it pops. We taste it when it is done. Add to the delight by looking and feeling. After the popcorn is popped, look at each piece with your grandchild. Look for shapes. Amazing things appear: little dogs and birds. Eat each piece one by one. Ask: "Is this something?" It can be just a glob! Add interesting toppings to the popcorn like soy sauce or grated cheese.

## Tea Party

There is magic in a tea party. Sometimes this special moment can be shared with Grandmother and grandchild. Sometimes other family members come. Serve something you do not usually eat—a special cookie or cracker or cinnamon toast. Use doll dishes or special tea party cups. Many cooking utensils can be found in miniature—tiny muffin tins and papers, tiny plates and bread-baking pans.

## Pizza

I am told that grandsons like to cook as well as granddaughters. One grandmother shared that creating pizzas is a favorite activity with her grandson. She makes the crust and her grandson creates the rest. Tomato sauce and cheese pizzas are his favorite.

**And here is another "kids' favorite" recipe your grandchildren might enjoy (Jeanne Kamrath and Sylverta Hill, teachers of three-year-olds at St. Luke's Day School in Houston, Texas, shared this recipe.):**

### Dinosaur Food

| | |
|---|---|
| 1/4 cup dirt (cocoa) | 1/2 cup swamp water (milk) |
| 1/2 cup fat (butter) | 2 cups crushed bones (sugar) |
| 2 cups grass (uncooked oatmeal) | |
| 1/2 cup squashed bugs (peanut butter) | |

Mix dirt and swamp water. Add crushed bones and fat. Heat to a boil. Add grass. Remove from heat. Add bugs. Place on waxed paper and cool. Eat and enjoy!

**Every family has their favorite recipes. My editor Melanie Grimes shared these recipes from her family:**

### Pecan Crunchies

| | |
|---|---|
| 1/2 box (16-oz.) graham crackers | 1/2 lb. butter |
| 1 cup dark brown sugar | 1 cup chopped pecans |

Lightly oil a jelly roll pan and line the bottom with whole graham crackers. Melt butter in a medium saucepan. Add brown sugar and stir until mixture bubbles vigorously. Add pecans and quickly spread over crackers. Bake at 350° for 10 minutes. Cut along indentations of crackers. Leave in pan and freeze for 1 hour. Break apart and refreeze in an airtight container. These goodies can be served right out of the freezer. Makes 4 dozen bars.

### 'Mom Cookies

| | |
|---|---|
| 1 cup butter, softened | 2 cups flour |
| 1/2 cup brown sugar | 1 tsp. ground cardamom |
| 1/2 cup sugar | 1/4 tsp. salt |
| 1 egg, separated | 1/3 cup chopped nuts |
| 1 tsp. almond extract | Butter Frosting (recipe below) |

Combine butter and sugars in mixing bowl. Beat until creamy and fluffy. Add egg yolk, vanilla, flour, cardamom and salt. Mix well to form a soft dough. Spread mixture in ungreased 10-by-15 inch baking pan. Brush surface with beaten egg white. Sprinkle evenly with nuts. Bake at 275° for 1 hour. Meanwhile prepare frosting: In skillet melt 1 1/2 tablespoon butter until butter browns slightly. Remove from heat. Beat in 1 cup powdered sugar and 1/2 teaspoon vanilla extract. Add enough milk to bring frosting to drizzling consistency. Drizzle frosting on warm cookies. Cut into 64 small bars.

### Summer Cake

| | |
|---|---|
| 1 1/2 cups flour | 8 oz. cream cheese, softened |
| 3/4 cup butter | 12 oz. whipped topping |
| 1 cup chopped nuts | 2 small pkgs. instant pudding |
| 1 cup powdered sugar | 3 cups milk |

Combine flour, butter and nuts in mixing bowl. Beat until a soft dough forms. Spread dough in 13-by-9-by-2 pan as a crust. Bake at 350° for 20 minutes. Combine cream cheese, powdered sugar and 1 cup whipped topping. Beat until smooth and then spread over cooled crust. Combine pudding mix ( I recommend lemon, pistachio, or chocolate) and milk and beat until smooth. Pour over cream cheese mixture. When firm, top with remaining whipped topping. Sprinkle with chopped nuts.

### Pistachio-Marshmallow Salad

| | |
|---|---|
| 12 oz. whipped topping | 20-oz. can crushed pineapple |
| 1/2 cups chopped nuts | 1 cup mini marshmallows |
| 1 small instant pistachio pudding | |

Mix all ingredients together and refrigerate.

### Banana & Peanut Butter Pancakes

| | |
|---|---|
| 1/4 cup peanut butter | 6 pancakes |
| 3 Tbsp. milk | 1 banana, sliced |
| 2 Tbsp. honey | |

In 1-cup microwave-safe measuring cup, combine peanut butter, milk and honey. Microwave on high for 30 to 45 seconds or until melted and smooth, stirring once halfway through cooking. Place banana slices evenly between layers and on top of pancakes. Pour peanut butter mixture over pancakes. Makes 2 servings.

# Grandmas

*Perkily*

Words and music by Mary Lu Walker

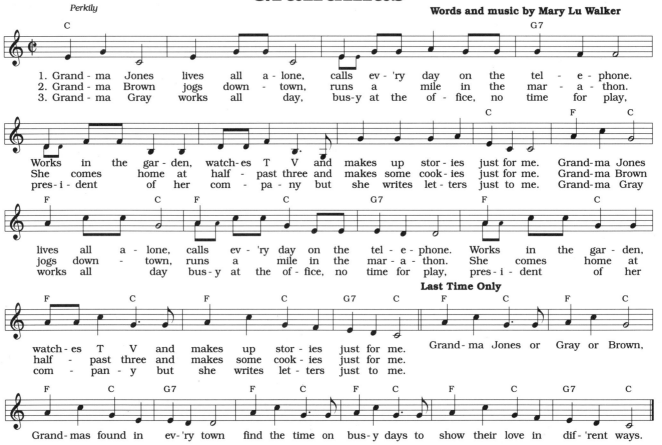

1. Grand - ma Jones lives all a - lone, calls ev - 'ry day on the tel - e - phone.
2. Grand - ma Brown jogs down - town, runs a mile in the mar - a - thon.
3. Grand - ma Gray works all day, bus - y at the of - fice, no time for play,

Works in the gar - den, watch - es T V and makes up stor - ies just for me. Grand - ma Jones
She comes home at half - past three and makes some cook - ies just for me. Grand - ma Brown
pres - i - dent of her com - pa - ny but she writes let - ters just to me. Grand - ma Gray

lives all a - lone, calls ev - 'ry day on the tel - e - phone. Works in the gar - den,
jogs down - town, runs a mile in the mar - a - thon. She comes home at
works all day bus - y at the of - fice, no time for play, pres - i - dent of her

**Last Time Only**

watch - es T V and makes up stor - ies just for me. Grand - ma Jones or Gray or Brown,
half - past three and makes some cook - ies just for me.
com - pan - y but she writes let - ters just to me.

Grand - mas found in ev - 'ry town find the time on bus - y days to show their love in dif - 'rent ways.